Writing
a
Jewish
Life

Memoirs

Lev Raphael

CARROLL & GRAF PUBLISHERS
NEW YORK

For those who guided me

WRITING A JEWISH LIFE
Memoirs

Carroll & Graf Publishers
An Imprint of Avalon Publishing Group Inc.
245 West 17th Street
11th Floor
New York, NY 10011

AVALON
publishing group incorporated

Copyright © 2006 by Lev Raphael

First Carroll & Graf edition 2006

"Writing a Jewish Life" appeared in *Tikkun*, "Writing Something Real" appeared in *Who We Are: On Being (and Not Being) an American Jewish Writer*, "Almost Famous?" appeared in different form in *The Third Degree*, "A Writer High and Low" was a keynote address at BEA and appeared in *Forward* on-line, and "Heart of Darkness" is forthcoming in *Wonderlands II*. "Okemos, Michigan," "Letter from Israel I & II," "Losing My Mother," "Selling Was Never My Line," "Scars," and "Judaism's Moral Strength" appeared in *Journeys & Arrivals*.

Library of Congress Cataloging-in-Publication Data is available.

ISBN: 0-7867-1649-5
ISBN-13: 978-0-78671-649-4

Printed in the United States of America
Interior design by Maria Elias
Distributed by Publishers Group West

Contents

Metamorphosis was the secret heart of life.
—Salman Rushdie, *Shalimar the Clown*

Author's Note

"Writing a Jewish Life" appeared in *Tikkun*, "Writing Something Real" appeared in *Who We Are: On Being (and Not Being) a Jewish American Writer*, "Almost Famous?" appeared in different form in *The Third Degree*, "A Writer High and Low" was a keynote address at BEA and appeared in *Foreword* on-line, and "Heart of Darkness" is forthcoming in *Wonderlands II*. "Okemos, Michigan," "Letter from Israel I & II," "Losing My Mother," "Selling Was Never My Line," "Scars," and "Judaism's Moral Strength" appeared in *Journeys & Arrivals*. These latter essays appeared some ten years ago, and I've left the references to time unchanged to keep them true to the moments of their inspiration. Since then, my sons, who are mentioned in two of the essays, have grown up, gotten married, and established flourishing lives of their own. I hope they won't mind that the essays have not caught up with them.

Writing a Jewish Life

I grew up in a minefield.

As a child of Holocaust survivors, I never knew when I might say or do the wrong thing and spark a devastating comment from my parents, something so dark and humiliating that I would feel as if the ground under me had exploded and a whirlpool had opened up and swallowed me alive.

Nothing could be wasted in our home, nothing could be thrown out. If I were scraping some unfinished food from my plate into the garbage can, I might be greeted with, "You know what we would have done for something like that in the war?"

No, I didn't know, not really, and I was afraid to ask, because I was wasting food when my parents had starved during the war. How could I be so thoughtless and cruel?

Of course, it was always "the war"—as if no other war had ever occurred in human history and no other tragedy had ever befallen the Jews. It was the air we breathed, the silence between words, the beast in the jungle waiting to spring. It was the horrible nightmares my father had, nightmares that had him crying out wordlessly, waking everyone up except himself. Their grip was so fierce that my mother had to shake and shake him to bring him back. I never knew the content of those dreams, just their coordinates: the war.

For me, growing up, there seemed no other significant experience in the world but that war, the one that had stolen from my parents their family, friends, home, their country, their past. There were no mementos of their lives in Europe before the war, hardly any photographs, even memories were in short supply because they were dangerous.

But there were mines, everywhere, waiting to explode.

Like the time when I was around eight years old, making a hand puppet from an old white sock on which I'd crayoned a face. He was going to be a superhero, so I tied a handkerchief around his neck to make the cape. But he needed an emblem, which I drew on his chest with gold glitter. A bolt of lightning. It looked so good, I drew a second one and showed it to my mother, expecting praise and smiles. I was the kind of kid whose school art projects were almost always misshapen—these even bolts of lightning were a real triumph for me.

"It's just like the SS insignia," she said. So the everyday scene of a child showing off his creation to a parent—played out tens of thousands of times in every family—was turned into a lesson of unpredictability and shame. It could happen any time, anywhere. Whatever I was proud of could set off an explosion, could take my mother or father away, could crush me into insignificance.

And there were more than just these spare and critical comments. There were flashes of something closer to narrative, like flares lighting up the scene of devastation on a battlefield, or eruptions of some smoldering volcano. Who can remember what set them off? A song on the radio, an article in the newspaper, even something in my homework. Anything. Everything.

Though I was a mouthy kid, I had no words with which to

respond. What can a child say when he's having after-school milk and cookies and somehow the war has joined him and his mother at the table, as inappropriate and ineluctable as death?

Even as an adolescent I was silenced. Once while frantically looking for my keys, I threw things around my room and left without picking up the huge mess on the floor. When I returned, my mother told me it was just like when the Nazis stormed into her house in 1941 and started tearing it apart.

Tolstoy famously wrote that "all happy families are like one another; each unhappy family is unhappy in its own way." But I think that doesn't hold true for families of Holocaust survivors, because we share a common landscape, the one that Lesbian Jewish poet Melanie Kaye/Kantrowitz described this way: "where i came from was / burned off the map."

What might be a little different is that my search for understanding of what happened to my parents, what had spoiled and twisted their lives and left me an inheritance of terrible ambivalence about being Jewish, led me to become a writer.

In other words: a traitor, a spy, a betrayer of family secrets.

How did it happen?

I was in love with storytelling from an early age. My mother read to me, but I learned to read by myself quite well and quite early—partly through studying the captions to photos in *Life* magazine—and I was also writing little stories myself. In second grade I discovered science fiction and wrote a story about an alien who landed on earth, looked around and didn't like what he saw, so he flew away. Surprise, surprise.

I was a stranger in a strange land, and I don't just mean America, I mean my family. Novelist Elizabeth Benedict puts it this way: "The living room. The most treacherous country of all." Even in second grade, I was trying to make sense of this alien territory that was home.

My parents spoke Yiddish and read a Yiddish newspaper, had Jewish friends, yet looked down on American Jews. Partly it was because they had done so little to help my parents when they immigrated to the United States in 1950 and had even failed to live up to promises of support, but mainly because to them, American Jews were inauthentic, a cheap imitation of the real thing. The real thing was the Jewish Atlantis, a lost and mythical Yiddish-speaking land that had been destroyed by catastrophe, burned off the map.

Even though my father kept his store open on Saturday, he and my mother made fun of the Reform rabbi who drove to the *shul* down the block and mocked the *ungemacht* (overdone) hats of the women going to services. "It's an Easter parade!" And my father often told variations of a joke I'm sure many people have heard. A woman asks her Orthodox rabbi to say a *brocha* over her new car and he refuses: "What are you, crazy? Who does such a thing?" She finds a Conservative rabbi and he also says no, but more politely. The Reform rabbi she locates is affable and says, "I'd be happy to—but first you have to tell me—what's a *brocha*?" That was my father's verdict on American Jews, the smiling disdain of a man who grew up in the same part of the world as Elie Wiesel but never set foot in a synagogue after the war.

For my multilingual mother, who prided herself on her literacy, the Yiddish she heard in America made her cringe. As she would be happy to inform you, she spoke a pure and literary Vilno Yiddish. What she encountered in the United States was no better than a Yiddish version of Brooklynese, or, you should excuse the expression, pig Latin.

My parents made me attend a Workmen's Circle Sunday school, but I never enjoyed it much. Why should I? Despite speaking Yiddish, these were people my parents didn't have an ounce of respect for, especially the ones who had offered my mother a job when they saw her work in Brussels but reneged on the promise. She had been teaching Yiddish literature at a Bund-organized school whose students were either survivors or hidden during the war. They thought she was terrific in 1947 in Brussels, but in 1950 New York they thought she was nobody. I'll never know why.

But I can still recall the way one of my younger teachers looked at her the first time they met, sometime in my early teens, her mouth slightly agape, clearly drinking in my mother's beautiful Yiddish with as much rapture as a Czarist Russian émigré meeting someone claiming to be Anastasia.

When my consciousness of Israel started to develop, I asked why they hadn't gone there after the war, and the answer was unswervingly angry from my mother: "Live with all those Jews! I had enough of them in the ghetto and the camps!" So—being with Jews, being Jewish itself did not seem something to be proud of. Worse, it was dangerous.

The war had stolen my parents' past, home, family, their

whole world, some of their pride, and even language. During the war my father for a long time had to pretend to be Christian, and he learned prayers so well that he forgot how to read Yiddish and had to be taught by my mother when they met after the war.

We had an uncle in Israel. There were pictures of him and his family. Why didn't my mother write to him? She didn't say it outright, but it had to be because he and her other brother had managed to escape from Vilno into Russia when the Nazis came, and she was left to take care of her parents. Left. A small word that covers an enormous tragedy. The five of them were on the last train from Vilno, but the Russians cleared it of Jews at the border. My mother's brothers ran after it, urging my mother and their parents to run, too, but they couldn't. And so the three of them made their way back to Vilno on foot, four hundred kilometers my mother said, with bombs falling around them. Take care of her parents? Impossible—the Nazis shot her father at Ponar and gassed her mother at Treblinka.

In first grade, perhaps around the time of the Eichmann trial, a girl at school told me that "they threw Jewish babies up in the air and caught them on bayonets." *This* was a people I wanted to identify with?

I don't think it's an accident that my favorite book as a little boy was *The Three Musketeers,* which I read over and over so many times that it annoyed my mother and the book's binding broke and frayed. It's a novel where swords are wielded not against infants but adults, a book where a solitary young man plunges into a tumultuous world of adventure, loyalty, betrayal, a world in which he triumphs. It's true that little boys often imagine themselves as powerful and daring because they are surrounded by giants, but for me this book had deeper resonance. I see now that it was a story of conquest, and the few stories that were emerging from my parents were anything but heroic, at least as a boy would understand them. My parents had been victims, people had tried to kill them. Later I would learn that it wasn't just—just!—the brutal machinery of Nazism that they faced.

My father had cheated death twice before being imprisoned in Bergen-Belsen. Once as a slave laborer in the Hungarian army when a Hungarian officer had lobbed a grenade at him and missed, a second time when he was standing in front of a firing squad and the RAF started bombing the area and he escaped. And he had cheated death a third time at the war's end when the train he was on from Bergen-Belsen was stopped by the U.S. Ninth Army, and the Jews crammed onto it were saved from being machine-gunned and thrown into the Elbe.

Though I was an extroverted and noisy child (my mother said that she always knew where I was in our large, rambling apartment), I spent much of my growing up deep inside books. From an early age, if I liked an author, I read everything that person had written, some of the books twice or even three times. Call it training to be a writer, call it escape. It served both purposes very well.

I read four or five books a week from the local library housed in a turn-of-the-century Gothic pile, always relishing my own choices over what was assigned at school, which was usually less interesting and less complex. For years I read science fiction and history, fascinated by alternate universes and by maps of Europe that showed vast territorial changes. Look at one page, a country exists. Turn the page to another century, and it's gone. I knew something about such disappearances.

I read obsessively about dolphins, about attempts to communicate with them. Of course I was interested in this kind of investigation—wasn't I living in a murky submarine world of my own, with connection out of reach?

But when I discovered Henry James in junior high, where an English teacher had assigned James's short novel *Washington Square,* something precious beckoned to me. Though I wouldn't have been able to express it at the time, this story of the shy, ungraceful daughter tyrannized by a contemptuous father struck home, struck a chord in my home. I knew what it was like to feel out of place, criticized, different at home and in the world.

It may be hard to remember, but the 1950s and 1960s were not remotely like the '70s—there was little open discussion of the Holocaust yet. As Alan Mintz has written in *Popular Culture and the Shaping of Holocaust Memory in America,* in the postwar celebration of victory over fascism, there was no room in America for this dark story without a happy ending. American Jews themselves were busy entering American society and making their mark, and for the most part they didn't want to hear what survivors had to say, so Holocaust survivors often felt stigmatized and silent. Survivors didn't have moral stature yet, and the whole subject was painful and embarrassing. I knew no better way to stop a discussion with my Jewish friends' parents than to say, "My parents were in concentration camps."

My parents were not only burned and branded by the past, resentful of the present in which money was extremely tight, and their suffering only seemed to count for something among their network of friends, who were all Holocaust survivors. My parents were angry, and it could erupt unexpectedly. With their wealth of languages between them—Yiddish, Russian, Polish, Czech, German, French, and more—they spoke English with embarrassingly heavy accents and could become enraged, in public, over what seemed to me to be trivialities. They embarrassed me, and in my grammar school classes I had the misfortune of being the only child of immigrants in a crowd of children whose parents were all comfortably bourgeois *yekkehs*. My classmates had large allowances, went to summer camps, joined the Boy Scouts, even traveled outside of New York for vacations. New England. Florida. California. These were all impossible for me.

A difficult environment to grow up in, but a rich field of observation, yet it remained buried treasure for years. I took creative writing courses in high school and college and discovered a stronger facility with language and imagery, with words, than I'd known I had. But my writing was as far away from myself as possible, and by that I mean as far away from my world, my own observations, my truest knowledge.

I was afraid of outrage and retribution both from non-Jews for being Jewish and from Jews for being either bisexual or gay. I had seen and studied the incredible uproar in the Jewish community generated by Philip Roth's *Portnoy's Complaint*, which was published as I entered adolescence. The book terrified me for its defiance of taboos, for its open shouting at Jewish fearfulness and restriction. Roth once observed that what really made the book so infamous is that no one expects a Jew to go crazy in public. Not Jews, and especially not non-Jews, who as Portnoy says, "own the world and know absolutely nothing about human boundaries."

This was not mere rhetoric to me, this was real. My parents had seen their neighbors in Poland and Czechoslovakia eliminate human boundaries. And so I was afraid not only of betraying *them*, but also of exposing myself to potentially hostile goyish eyes. No wonder my fiction was full of disguises. It read like a series of desperate flares sent up for help.

But my creative writing professor in college understood those flares and kept encouraging me to write something real. And even though I shared with her my confused sexuality, it took until my senior year before I was ready to begin claiming my talent as a writer. I was deeply in love with a non-Jewish girl who wanted to marry me, and the many layers of conflict were boiling over.

I needed her. I loved her. She loved Christmas—could I have a Christmas tree in our future home? It seemed impossible. Every time I walked down an imaginary road to our life together, I stumbled. What about our children? I knew nothing about how to raise a Jewish child, but I couldn't stomach the idea of raising a non-Jewish one. It would make me even less connected, less authentic, less me.

That was the year I read Henry James's *The Portrait of a Lady* and finally found an entrance into myself. It's a story of a free-spirited, independent, optimistic woman who finds that a huge inheritance leads into the blind alley of a loveless, cold marriage. Understanding at last the nature of her trap, she sits in front of a fire, mulling over what her life has come to, realizing that her imagined home of free expression and love openly given and received is really "The house of dumbness, the house of deafness, the house of suffocation."

I read that passage at three in the morning and was never the same again. That was the house I lived in. I saw it, felt it, finally had the words.

For several years my writing professor had urged me to write something real. Now I was ready. My writing started to take on an emotional depth and color that was new, and not much later I began a story that was completely unlike anything I'd ever written before. It opened with a paragraph describing a character's father and how the boy felt around him. I knew it was the doorway into a story I had to tell—and was afraid to tell. After I called my writing professor and read it to her on the phone, she urged me to keep writing, in fact made me agree to write a section, call her and read it to her, write another, call her, and so on until it was done a day and a half later. I was terrified—I was alive.

It turned into a story about the son of Holocaust survivors who felt alienated by his parents' past and crushed by it.

I was in a graduate writing program at the time, and my workshop group, including the professor, hated it. They took turns dissecting it for an hour or so, and then the professor disdainfully picked through the remains and pronounced it worthless. Did that mean anything? A *simn a loksh ofn bord,* as they say in Yiddish. The story won a prestigious writing prize judged by a famous editor and was published in *Redbook,* which had four and a half million readers. I made a lot of money and I received fan mail, realizing for the first time the power of being able to touch someone with what you write.

My parents were not touched, they were angry and disappointed. They had tried in their own way to shield me from the Holocaust, and here I was writing about it—and them—in disguised ways, and writing about my own feelings. I wasn't supposed to *have* any feelings. My brother helpfully told me not to do it again.

I was devastated by their criticism, but I wasn't silenced. Winning the prize and getting published had given me more than enough positive feedback on my work to feel emboldened to keep writing. I couldn't turn back, but realized their approval was not a prize to long for. After all, as Janet Malcolm says, "Art is theft. Art is armed robbery. Art is not pleasing your mother."

Writing the story led me to consciously confront my troubled legacy as a child of survivors, and for the first time I started to read furiously about the Holocaust, steeping myself now in what for years had merely been bits of narrative gleaned from my parents, conquering my own nausea and fear of entering that Kingdom of Death. The timing couldn't have been better. It was 1979 and Helen Epstein had made headlines with her book *Children of the*

Holocaust. Holocaust curricula were being introduced all over the United States, and Gerald Green's miniseries "Holocaust" was filling America's TV screens.

I think that we children of Holocaust survivors may tend to feel we know a lot about those nightmare years in Europe, given the way they have left an imprint on our parents. But like many others, I actually knew little in the way of facts before I began reading hundreds of articles and books of all kinds, and I came to see that I had wanted to know less, because the Holocaust had stolen my parents' past not just from them but from me and had made reminiscing a dangerous and bleak prospect. This reading led me to teach a soul-stirring course in the Holocaust at the school in New York where I was an adjunct professor and made me contemplate the role of my writing as serving a larger social purpose, as opposed to being my individual path to success.

That's why the next five or six years were particularly frustrating. I was unable to sell a single story, anywhere. Rejections seemed to come by the pound. Perhaps I was young and overconfident and suffering from New York fantasies of greatness. Perhaps people weren't as ready to read fiction about the Second Generation as I had thought. I'll never know. What I do know is that it took being transplanted to Michigan—where I went to do a PhD—to end the drought.

A black friend had told me she never felt so black as when she moved from New York City to Michigan, and I have to tell you that East Lansing made me feel very Jewish. I, who had never been to a Passover Seder until I was twenty-three, sought out High Holy Day services for only the second time in my life. I moved into a Jewish students co-op. I found myself attending Orthodox services, and the feeling of sitting there for hours every Shabbat was like being wrapped in a warm and life-giving tallis.

This shift had begun in New York before I left, because the overwhelming immersion in reading about the Holocaust, about how Jews had died in Europe from 1933 to 1945, had left me hungry to know how they had lived. Though I'd read books of Jewish history before, I knew nothing about Judaism, and so I turned to books like Abraham Heschel's *The Earth Is the Lord's* and Milton Steinberg's *Basic Judaism*. I found myself proud of my religion, and fascinated by it.

So people at the minyan helped me learn prayers, learn what they meant, learn the structure of the services so that I could feel at home, and they invited me into their homes and taught me what it was like to make Shabbat a refuge from the week. The first time I lit Shabbat candles in my little room, I had truly crossed a boundary and become a *baal tshuvah*. That same year I held the Torah during Kol Nidre, chanted by a Holocaust survivor with all the passion of a professional Old World cantor. I felt exalted and faint—and that night I dreamt that someone was singing *Av harachamim*—merciful father. Isn't that what I needed?

Michigan—which we Jews there like to call the land of *michigoyim*—had other surprises for me. I met a nice Jewish doctor—with two sons. Not exactly what my parents had hoped for. I had supposed that they would cut me some slack because my brother had married a Catholic whom me mother called a *"Poylisheh dripkeh,"* but we were both considered disappointments.

My partner had grown up with Orthodox Judaism forced on him without explanations. Whenever he'd ask why something was done, the answer was always "because." Well, together we started exploring how to connect ourselves to Jewish life, and I'm happy to say that our growing devotion to Yiddishkeit in many forms had a profound impact on one of my stepsons, who is now a Hillel director.

This involvement with Jewish observance, which had been totally foreign to me, also led me to ask a simple question: if I truly had something to say, who was my audience? At the time I'd been trying to publish in national and literary magazines—but what about Jewish publications? *Andekt America,* right?

That was clearly the answer, and through the 1980s I steadily published again in places like the *Baltimore Jewish Times,* the *Detroit Jewish News, Agada, Reconstructionist, Hadassah,* and even a Jewish magazine called *Shmate.*

By 1990 I was ready to publish a book of stories, *Dancing on Tisha B'Av,* whose subjects are children of survivors, coming out, anti-Semitism, and homophobia. It was the first book of its kind and generated a great deal of interest and many invitations to speak, though I'm sorry to say, none from Jewish book fairs. They wouldn't decide I was kosher until the mid-1990s, and people would nervously ask me, "Can I give this book to my rabbi?"

I started touring bookstores and synagogues around the country and was amazed at the outpouring of gratitude for my work—and by the stories people told me. Quite often they were about secrets, about how individuals had found out they were Jewish in extraordinary circumstances.

I felt called. I recast a novel I'd been working on for years as a novel about secrets. *Winter Eyes* tells the story of Polish Jews who not only leave Europe but leave their Jewishness behind, or try to. They raise their son, Stefan, as a Catholic, and the book charts the price of hiding in this family. Of all my books, it may have earned me the most impassioned personal comments.

After that novel I was drawn in different directions—children's literature, psychology and education, memoir, a book about Edith Wharton, but always filled by a sense of discovery and mission, feeling that each book was important, had something to offer, something to say. This was more than just the average writer's feeling of importance and healthy self-regard.

If it sounds a bit heavy and serious, it was. The years of writing and speaking about the Holocaust and its impact had worn me out, and I needed a break. I also felt that my sense of humor never found expression in my work, and that was troubling. So in the mid-1990s I turned to writing mysteries. These were not just any mysteries, but academic satirical mysteries with a Jewish gay protagonist. That's probably niche marketing at its finest.

My amateur sleuth's partner was the character who appeared as a child and teenager in *Winter Eyes,* so there was a thread of Second Generation anxiety and pain even there, and an attempt to deal with Jewish identity. What I write, whether serious or not, will always be imbued with a sense of purpose, and, being Jewish, not just in subject matter but in its sense of urgency to break every constricting silence. Jews have always been enjoined to tell their stories: The Book of Amos says, "Tell your children of it." Telling our stories keeps memory alive, builds bridges between communities, helps people find pride in their identity, and breaks the hold of silence.

But twenty-three years as a published writer have taught me that publishing is a hazardous enterprise at best, an arena of life where it would be best to inject your self-esteem with novocaine if such a thing were possible. A career is as unpredictable as the stock market, exhilarating on some days, crushing on others. Having something to say doesn't mean that people will necessarily listen, or more accurately, that you will be able to get past the gate-keepers, the editors who act like sheep, afraid to tackle something new or risky.

Still, you go on despite the obstacles. I think that I was born with the skill to be a writer, and that my talent was forged in response to my parents' suffering and loss in the war, and my own confusion and pain in response to theirs. These past two decades of writing have made it clear that no matter how suc-cessful I am, my success will not redeem my parents' pain, but only my own. I think this is a realization that many children of survivors have to come to. The infamy that struck our parents' lives can't be erased by our fame, however great. That doesn't diminish what we've accomplished; it only sets it in a more realistic context. When I look back at my beloved *Three Musketeers*, I see there is as much sorrow as excitement, as much pain as romance. The book isn't just a stage for swaggering swordplay—it is filled with loss, betrayal, loneliness, and death. Yet D'Artagnan survives with his honor intact. He grows up.

My career as a writer has deepened my Jewishness in surprising ways, brought wonderful new people into my life, and has made me stay alert to the unexpected—the idea for a book that suddenly appears out of nowhere, bringing a whole new set of pressures and delights.

My latest project brings me back to that kitchen table where I sat with my mother after school. It's something I feel as called to write as anything that's ever seized my imagination and stirred my dreams, and it has opened my word hoard, as the Anglo-Saxon poets used to say.

After the war, my parents met in a displaced persons camp and wound up in Belgium. My mother, from a prominent Bundist family in Vilna, became a teacher at that Bund school in Brussels I mentioned before, whose students were child survivors of the Holocaust or Jewish children hidden in Belgium by priests and nuns and other citizens. The Belgians did a particularly fine job of hiding Jews, especially Jewish children. But these children had lost not just years of schooling, they had lost their connection to Yiddishkeit, and my mother taught Yiddish language and literature in an atmosphere of safety, love, and excitement. From what I have gathered, these were extraordinary times. People were alive again, and Brussels was a small *gan eyden*, a paradise, after the sufferings of the war.

My mother always spoke fondly, joyfully of this time in her life, of the bakery on the first floor of their building where the scent of early morning breads wafted them awake, of the squeaky tram line on their street, of the delicious fresh vegetables they couldn't seem to find in New York, of the oddities and humor of living in a bicultural and bilingual country. They lived in Anderlecht and my father learned Flemish, while my mother's prewar French flourished.

I heard about the plays her students performed, I saw her look at photos of them with affection and longing. She had kept the going-away present she had been given—a gorgeous clutch leather bag—wrapped and untouched. She loved her students, and in researching a book about this school and this special time of rebirth, I have been searching for and finding some of them. My mother's favorite student lives in Melbourne, but I've been able to interview her in Brussels and Houston.

This book may take years. There are people I need to interview face-to-face in Los Angeles, Montreal, Toronto, Brussels, Melbourne. I'm eager to contact those elderly survivors whose insight and recollections I need, though I also know this is a complex story that cannot be rushed. It is a book I was born to write, combining memoir, travelogue, history, psychology. It will be a journey and a joy.

For me, writing has proven to be a catalyst, a laboratory. It has led to a deepened Jewish consciousness, profound connections with my people, building bridges between Jew and non-Jew, gay and straight. It has healed my own inner world and it has been *tikkun olam*. I want everything I write to say in one way or another what

Jews say after someone has had an honor during a Torah service, *yasher koach*—may your strength be multiplied.

And that is especially true in these troubling times.

It's impossible to talk about these issues without referring to what happened in September 2001 in New York.

One consistent thread in firsthand accounts of the Holocaust I've read is the response to shocking news, and particularly the news about the concentration camps.

In memoir after memoir, report after report, one hears of Jews who were trapped in ghettoes or in hiding saying, "It can't be true. It's not possible." People didn't behave like that. Germans *couldn't* behave like that—they were so civilized, so cultured. My parents were among those who doubted the truth; it was simply too grotesque.

Initial accounts in American newspapers of Nazi atrocities were greeted with disbelief, as Walter Laqueur described in his book *The Terrible Secret*. And when the Polish representative Jan Karski—an eyewitness to the operation of the Belzec concentration camp—came to America to report what was happening in Poland, Justice Felix Frankfurter told him, "I can't believe you." He did not think that Karski was lying; he simply could not assimilate the unimaginable.

On the morning of Tuesday, September 11, I stayed by the TV from the moment my youngest stepson called to tell me the World Trade Center was on fire and a plane had hit one of the towers. And even though I saw the second plane hit and then heard the news about the Pentagon, I quite literally could not believe what I was seeing. I'd just been in New York a day before and had flown past the World Trade Center through clear skies.

When my stepson said, "Oh my God, the tower's collapsing," my first thought was, "It's on fire. The smoke and dust is from the fire."

Only later did I realize that despite the evidence of my eyes, my stepson's alarm, and the reports from commentators on the scene, I had immediately sought a less painful truth. Even though I had television, like Jews around the world during World War II facing the growing evidence of Nazi genocide, I was vainly searching for a ray of hope.

When the first plane hit, my father was only three blocks away from the World Trade Center. Had circumstances been a little different, he might have been right on the scene and his car might have been one of the dusty shattered hulks whose images have filled the news.

"Don't ask," he said. "It was like the war. The explosions—"

It was the fourth time in his life that he escaped death.

Feeling the shock, feeling the sense of violation, terror, but particularly the disbelief that has hit New Yorkers and the country as a whole, it is only now, some fifty-odd years after my parents arrived in this free country, that I have a real inkling of what it must have felt like to say during the Holocaust, "This can't be happening. It's not possible." I feel closer to what my parents went through, in a strange and horrible way.

The unimaginable has come home, which makes the world all the more in need of healing, and writing.

Okemos, Michigan

We were just looking—that's all I had agreed to.

Ten years ago, I had reluctantly said I would "look," after Gersh had called while I was at a conference in San Francisco. He told me that we should buy a house in Okemos (where we had separate apartments) instead of trying to rent one, because there weren't many rentals available just then in Okemos, near East Lansing. I felt both sick and stunned at the idea of owning a house, let alone our actually living together, and the day after he called, I came down with the flu.

I had grown up in Washington Heights, a hilly and park-filled upper Manhattan neighborhood as remote to many New Yorkers as Riverdale or even Albany, though it's now infamous for the cocaine sales and murders scarring its shaded boulevards and Depression-era buildings. Back then, I thought of houses as completely alien, out in the suburbs, something to visit or drive by. And I pictured them as negatively as Birkin did in *Women in Love*: "'the world all in couples, each in its own little house, watching its own little interests, and stewing in its own little privacy—it's the most repulsive thing on earth.'"

But Indian Hills, the Okemos subdivision in which we looked at a third house one sunny May morning, was not at all repulsive. It is an oak-lined neighborhood of about two hundred houses, a few miles from Michigan State University in East Lansing, with curving streets; old blue spruces, maples, scotch pines, towering arbor vitae, weeping willows, and magnolias; overgrown yew hedges and shrubs; lots of nearly an acre; and thirty- or forty-year-old houses set well back from the road. While there are some large homes, this is not the wealthiest part of a prosperous and stoutly Republican suburb studded with Michigan State faculty members, but dominated by Lansing-area professionals whose wives wear mink and drive Cutlass Cierras, Jaguars, and an occasional Porsche. The houses in Indian Hills are not at all pretentious, like the newer, Tudoresque homes in nearby subdivisions that dwarf their tiny lots.

Indian Hills is even more appealing given that a few minutes away you could be in any featureless part of the homogenized Midwest, swamped by malls and mini-malls, wholesale outlets, fast food and video encampments, and grim acres of parking lots. Best of all, the day we saw our house, we drove off East Lansing's and Okemos's main street, Grand River Avenue, to cross a narrow bridge into the subdivision. The road curved around the neighborhood's nine-hole golf course, which was studded with groups of shirtless hunky young MSU students as picturesque as classical statuary on an English lord's estate. "Beautiful," I murmured. And it all was, though the four-bedroom house we stopped at looked like a simple ranch from outside. It was fronted at the street by a ginkgo tree, which I recognized from its fan-shaped leaves because one had grown in the park near my elementary school in Inwood. Finding the ginkgo and having crossed the bridge made me feel I had entered some childhood fantasy.

Nearer the house was an enormous flowering tree in full bloom, whose wide-spreading boughs started from just a few feet above the ground; the blossoms were fuschia, edged with white. I discovered it was a hawthorn, the first one I had ever had pointed out to me, and so, like a child learning the word *table*, I felt suddenly possessed of mysterious but useful information.

Years before this morning, in New York, I had gone apartment hunting with my college writing teacher and best friend Kris, and we had unexpectedly and angrily fled from one with a sumptuous view of the Hudson because the apartment made us feel very anxious. "This is an *awful* place," Kris said, confused by the intensity of her feeling. "Something *terrible* happened here!" It did feel awful, almost possessed, but this house on Chippewa Drive in Okemos felt welcoming and warm. From a brick-walled vestibule, we stepped into a large open living room/dining room (the "great room") with a stone fireplace at one end. The long wall with large windows facing the back was not parallel to the one opposite it, and neither was a wall in the dining area, yet somehow these anomalies were delightful.

Gersh and I looked at each other and kept looking as we moved through the house, which was bigger and deeper than it had seemed from the street, and far more beautiful. The colors throughout were royal blue, maroon, beige, and orange and kept appearing in varying combinations in shades, curtains, custom-made rugs. Our tiny, tipsy-sounding realtor with big hair explained it was a "red-ribbon house"—you could move right in without having to change or prepare anything. That expression made me think of a contest capped by prizes and applause.

Each room drew us into the next. Details kept bursting on us like fireworks: the Italian tiles in the kitchen, exquisite fabric on the living room walls, honey-colored pine in the room I knew would be my study because it faced that glorious hawthorn in the front yard. We were falling in love not just with the house, but with the *idea* of ourselves there, with the idea of a home. We fit in. We looked at it twice more that day, brought Gersh's two sons over to see what they thought (since they would be spending about half their time with us), we looked at each other and said yes, and we made our offer that evening.

Gersh had wanted to live with me for years, but I had never believed it was possible—not because I doubted that gay men could live loving and happy lives together, but partly because Michigan, and more particularly the East Lansing area, had already become my home as an outwardly straight man, and I was unprepared to make the shift, to emerge, to give up my "anonymity." I had come to Michigan in 1981 ostensibly to do a doctorate, but really to escape my family, and, more important, to escape New York. It was a city I no longer had the courage or patience to live in: dirtier, noisier, more crowded and dangerous than the city I had assumed was the center of the universe when I was growing up. Two and a half years in bucolic Amherst, Massachusetts, had shown me I could flourish outside New York.

I fell in love with Michigan when I got here, exploring MSU's lush and spreading campus, traveling around the state with its more than three thousand miles of Great Lakes shoreline, up to Hemingway country, to Lake Michigan, Lake Huron, the Keweenaw peninsula, crossing the Mackinac (pronounced Mackinaw) Bridge at sunset. Life seemed simpler here, less oppressive, more inviting; like Joni Mitchell's free man in Paris, here in Michigan, "I felt unfettered and alive." Of course, being a graduate student is a strange mix in which the elements of servitude are often masked by romanticism, but even as I was finishing my degree, I knew that I would want to stay here: People were friendlier and more relaxed, without the defensive "walls" that most cities demand for survival. And most importantly, I could write here. In the mid-eighties, I had finally begun to feel that I had a career as a writer, and an audience.

Gersh was also a transplanted New Yorker (we had gone to the same high school, ten years apart) and felt about Michigan as I did. But having already made his great plunge into the future through divorce, he was ready and eager for a complete life together. The most I had previously agreed to was getting an apartment in the same complex he lived in. No one would see us, I thought. And here was the other side of living in Okemos: visibility. There were no crowds to lose yourself in. So, this sudden about-face, the abruptness of my decision to say yes to the house, to our living together, was all the more astonishing for both of us.

When we finally moved into the house, I was paranoid about being observed every time we were out in the enormous back yard with its two sassafras trees, sugar maples, and red oaks, or trimming hedges in the front, or even walking to the front door with groceries. In New York, neighbors had seemed tamer, less intrusive, even though they were sometimes just on the other side of a wall. You chatted with them in elevators or lobbies, at the mailboxes, but their scrutiny was something I rarely thought of. Here, I felt exposed and vulnerable, and it didn't help that every year when Gay Pride day came along, letters in MSU's student newspaper and the *Lansing State Journal* condemned homosexuality with unswerving hatred that masked itself as Christian love and salvation. Gersh tried to calm my anxieties with jokes, but it turned out that I was right. We *were* being watched, although not in the way I had imagined.

As we began shaping the house to become our own, we started a series of changes that kept escalating like those five-year plans in the former Soviet Union. After fruitless attempts to trim back the overgrown yews that hulked at practically every corner of the house, we started having them removed. Then we began replanting. My world expanded as we became habitués of local greenhouses and entered a community of gardeners. Each conversation I had about soil conditions, or sunlight, pests, drought stress, or winter kill marked how different this world was for me. I began to worry about how certain shrubs were doing, consulting books and experts. Plants became a permanent and enjoyable part of my conversation as I began to feel at home with them, and with the soil under my fingernails after an afternoon of planting.

The new and more interesting evergreens we planted at the front of the house, under the study window in a raised, stonededged bed, got our neighbors' attention. On either side of us and across the street lived elderly men and women, and all remarked on how well we were taking care of the house, especially that we were raking the leaves in the fall and not letting them scatter onto someone else's lawn. The lawn itself was a frequent subject of conversation. The previous owners had left it alone, which meant in the summer it was seared, thin, brown, and the rest of the year not much better, but we hired a lawn care firm and then installed an underground sprinkling system. People walking by on a nice day, from several streets over, would remark on the lovely changes in the property. They *had* been watching. And I realized I did the same. As we drove into or out of Indian Hills, I found myself intensely aware of changes in people's yards, new plantings, remodelings, and problems with a tree or shrub. I was becoming deeply connected to this place.

We also began changes in the house itself. And each alteration—whether it was new locks, a French door between the vestibule and the living room, or the entirely remodeled master bathroom and new roof—had the effect of making me feel more stable, more rooted, more secure. All of this was as exciting as working outdoors on the trees and shrubs because I had always lived in rental apartments, which stayed essentially the same no matter how creatively I moved my furniture around.

The greatest change was adding a deck onto what had been a scruffy screen porch, and having the porch itself enclosed, heated, and made into a sunroom. The large windows let in the outside but also made the house more open. I was growing less afraid of that, after we had taken out the grim chain-link fence the previous owners kept because of their dogs. This whole experience was a profound new reality for me. In just two years we had stripped the house bare of its ugly, obscuring yews, and opened up the back yard to the unexpected: a dog wandering through, utility repairmen up on their poles, the glances of strangers in other yards.

This was *my* house. I could do what I wanted. I could be what I wanted. If we hugged or held hands on the deck, it was our business and no one else's. Owning a house and creating a home had the entirely unexpected effect of making me gradually more proud, aggressive, more determined to be "out," to overcome the years of silence and lies. I see now that living in an apartment, or even renting a home would have continued the climate of hiding because the front door opens into transience. Here, I felt committed to living in this place, to voting for a board of supervisors that would slow the rate of growth in our township, to signing petitions about road closures or recycling, to writing letters to local officials so that my voice would be heard. I cared about the environment in this beautiful neighborhood—so quiet you could always hear the mourning doves or the chickadees—in ways I never could have cared in New York because someone else would be responsible there, surely.

If I had previously felt suspicious or hostile toward the idea of living in a house, perhaps part of what fueled my distance was the inevitable image of children. With only a few isolated moments of longing, I had never wanted to be a father, yet that's what I became when we moved in together, because Gersh shared custody of his two sons with his ex-wife, who lives a few minutes away. He was determined to stay in Okemos after his divorce so that he could be near his boys and so they could easily travel to and from school from either parent's home with minimum disruption. Both boys knew me and seemed to like me, but the bonds that developed between us when we started to live together became as powerful as my connection to the physical in my environment.

In the past ten years, my sense of time has shifted radically, and I am much more attuned to the seasons, as well as to the stages of a life. I eagerly note the first crocuses of spring and feel comforted by the smell of burning leaves in the fall, just as I've been aware of the boys getting taller, filling out, leaving the whining of childhood behind for the testing of adolescence, the burdens of young adulthood.

It was David, the elder boy, who at fourteen started talking about doing things "as a family"—a term that Gersh and I were determined not to force on him or Aaron, his younger brother. David wanted to go out to eat, all four of us, and to play board games and card games, especially ones he was good at. Many nights we played hours of hearts, and as with any family, each game recalled wild jokes and terrific plays of previous games. It was clear to me that we were building a history together.

Gradually, I was drawn into the boys' lives and have become an acknowledged "third parent" for them. It started with my helping with their homework, especially their writing assignments, and then running errands for them or with them—to their mother's house, to the mall, into town, to a friend's, or just going for a ride. Having another adult in the house made parenting a lot easier for Gersh, because he didn't have to be the only one the kids relied on. Having "backup" has been particularly valuable in family arguments because we can break down into teams, and someone always seems to be reasonable and in control, able to act as a sounding board.

Each year has brought new levels of closeness, as with David telling me things he asks me not to share with his father, or coming in after school and chatting about his day. He has told me that those chats have been the high point of each day, a chance for the two of us to get to know each other outside of the constraints of the group. Aaron and I have gone out by ourselves to see movies or shop, and my feelings for the boys have been a surprise. Talking to people who don't know me, I often reply to a comment about their children with, "Yes, my son does that too." The first time I mentioned this to the boys, they seemed very pleased. They can't have been too surprised, though, because we've all shared a great deal in ten years. We've had season tickets for the football team and even went out to the Rose Bowl in 1988 when Michigan State was the Big Ten champion (and beat USC!). We have taken short trips together, seen rock concerts, plays, and musicals at MSU's concert hall and elsewhere, gone on college visits, and Gersh and I have helped with their writing for school and on applications.

There have been other, unexpected connections between us.

Two years ago, Gersh and I went to a Rosh Hashanah service partly led by Aaron. It had been a year of explosive growth for

Aaron as a Jew. The catalysts were his deep involvement with the Greater Lansing Temple Youth, his attendance at several statewide conclaves for Jewish youth, and his time at the national Jewish leadership academy. Aaron was wondering what God meant to him, finding his place as a Jew, and not least, learning the guitar to be a song leader. His father and I marveled at his maturity and thoughtfulness in this search.

Gersh and I and about thirty others, mostly teenagers, attended a one-hour Rosh Hashanah service at our synagogue, and it was far more than we had anticipated: dynamic, moving, passionate, and personal.

Instead of a stage and an enormous hall, there was a small disheveled classroom decorated with travel posters for Israel, and an aleph bet chart. Instead of hundreds of people, many bored and chatting, there were only dozens, all singing and intent. Instead of distance, there was intimacy. The "creative service" started with a story about a simple shepherd who couldn't pray, but offered up his music to God. That is what I felt we were doing. The melodies of the prayers—many by the innovative Jewish writer Debbie Friedman—were warm and embracing, and often on the point of tears, I felt the transcendence that I hope to feel at services, but seldom experience except at nontraditional Jewish groups like Simcha, the Detroit-area organization for Jewish gays and lesbians Gersh and I belong to. Even more, the story of the shepherd, for me, included all those Jews who either don't have the Jewish education to feel fully comfortable at a service, and those who feel, as I did that morning, the futility of words.

I was incredibly proud of Aaron, who led services with the other guitar players as if he had been doing so for years. He was confident, smooth, relaxed, and smiling, his eyes connecting with those in the room again and again, his voice blending skillfully with the other two song leaders. His father and I were aglow with pride in Aaron's Jewish commitment and his newfound talent.

Afterward, I told Aaron what a gift he had, and how this service had connected my heart and my head. And in words my mother would have used, I told him that he surely had a *"yiddishe neshomah,"* a Jewish spirit.

All the parents attending were similarly moved and delighted. One commented, "That was the Jewish future in there."

Melodies from the service drifted through my head the rest of the day, and I felt at peace. It was totally unexpected, but completely welcome because I had come to the service in deep pain.

Almost a year before, my mother sunk into paranoia, terrifying confusion and violence that could only be controlled by heavy doses of drugs that left her quietly smiling and inoffensive. I wondered who was really there now behind the chemical wall that doctors felt was the only response to her multi-infarct dementia, a stroke-caused disease that looks very much like Alzheimer's. Off drugs today, my mother no longer recognizes anyone, never speaks, and is barely present. My father was inconsolable, my brother and I stunned, despairing.

Sitting in our temple on the eve of Rosh Hashanah (the day before we attended the service Aaron led), I rebelled as soon as I opened up *Gates of Repentance* and read about God's power and mercy.

Mercy?! How could God be called merciful when my mother had suffered through the unspeakable agonies of concentration camps, and was now deprived of her sense, cut off from her husband of almost forty years, from her children, from herself? I felt bitter, restless, incensed. The service felt like an unscalable cliff wall. God seemed intolerably far from me that night, and I felt the past was bearing down on me. Driving away later, I knew that these were age-old feelings and questions, but the continuity of doubt and pain did not console me.

And then the next morning—unexpectedly—I felt healed, thanks largely to Aaron and his music.

Having two children living with us, and feeling ourselves a family, has also unexpectedly helped ground me in the reality of my own identity as a gay man. I have found myself explaining news items to the kids about gay rights, sharing my outrage over Jesse Helms and other troglodytes—in other words, letting them know what moves and alarms me. I am a news addict, and both boys have become used to watching the evening news and talking about it, asking questions. David's intense interest in current events led to his majoring in international relations at the University of Wisconsin at Madison, then spending a year abroad at the University of Warwick in England. Aaron's social consciousness has expressed itself in deep involvement with environmental activities at his high school.

Living with people who love me has had the effect of making my freedom at home more precious, and the public opprobrium gays and lesbians deal with every day more pernicious.* Gersh and I are

---

*Having the quality of destroying or injuring.

not shy about being affectionate with each other, nor do we keep our involvement in gay causes secret. If anything, we have been convinced that modeling a healthy, committed, and politically aware and active relationship between two men is crucial. How we live has the potential to be a message to the boys that will hopefully override the sick and destructive messages about gays that they are bombarded with by their peers and by our culture.

The sense of security and family we feel has propelled us into an unexpected series of activities. Gersh and I were founding members of a study group of faculty and staff at Michigan State University that met regularly with the aim of establishing a gay and lesbian studies program at the university. We were also founding members of a Lansing-area coalition of gay and lesbian groups meeting to bridge the various gaps between the two communities and to develop joint political action. Both groups have convened at our house on various occasions, and the kids were well-informed of their aims. Gersh has offered a workshop at MSU's Counseling Center on self-esteem for gay men and has codeveloped and cotaught Michigan State's first course in gay and lesbian studies. We are both committed to making Lansing and Michigan more open, more accepting, and more protective of lesbians and gay men—because this is our home, and we cannot accept anything less. That has led to many letters and editorials for our campus paper, for the *Detroit Jewish News,* and the *Lansing State Journal.*

When Gersh and I first met, marveling at how much we had in common, our home was the world of ideas, because we started writing articles and then a book together. Everything we have co-authored has been published, and our joint teaching and lecturing has likewise been as powerful for our students and audiences as for us—knitting us together, creating a world of shared experiences. All of that laid a foundation for living together and ultimately making Okemos prove to us what Elizabeth Bowen says in her novel *The Death of the Heart* that "home is where we emotionally live."

Letter from Israel, I

I

The sun seemed to burn all sound off the long slow waves licking and foaming in pantomime. I sat far back from the water, staring. Tomorrow, my third day at a kibbutz on the Mediterranean, I would no longer be a "guest of the kibbutz." After sunrise, I would start painting newly built apartments. I had spent just a week in Israel, staying with an aunt and uncle outside Tel Aviv. I'd toured Jerusalem, the Negev, Caesaria, Masada, the Dead Sea. For now, my traveling was over.

Somewhere behind me I heard the thick guttural voices of the Dutch women. Most of the kibbutz volunteers were from the Netherlands or Scandinavia; they had come as soon as the Yom Kippur War of 1973–1974 was over and had stayed on. Two large Swedish women lived in the tin-roofed shack next to mine. They did peculiar calisthenics out in front, eyeing me with clinical disapproval whenever I passed. I was so skinny and undeveloped. Many of the volunteers spoke English, as did the kibbutzniks, but I had not come to Israel to talk, or to think.

I stroked sand from my thighs, picked up my towel, and made my way up the slope to the kibbutz's well-planted cliff line. In my small damp room, I sank onto the battered cot to nap before dinner, but my roommate Roberto, a Brazilian Jew, came in from the showers and took a long time drying his red-brown body. I squeezed my eyes shut. Slim, boyish, incongruously blue-eyed, he had the poignant dark perfection of an angel in a Renaissance fresco, from dense Botticelli curls to slim, incredibly high-arched and delicate feet.

The night before, he had invited me to walk on the beach: "The moon . . ." he sighed. But I had read on in the Jane Austen paperback I'd bought in Tel Aviv, reassured by the book's rhythms, which cooled me more than the jerky little shelf fan could. At night, the shack's walls, grimy with abandoned posters, snapshots, and a crumbling papier-mâché mask were not so lonely to look at. The unfamiliar sea whisper almost convinced me I was getting somewhere.

I had abruptly fled the meltdown of a messy menage à trois in bucolic western Massachusetts for ten days in Israel. As a child of concentration camp survivors, I had family nowhere else in the world, so Israel was the one destination for which I could make a call, buy a ticket, and leave within a week of the slightly hysterical decision—knowing I'd find some kind of home when I got there.

And Israel was far enough away for me to feel a vicious sense of satisfaction when I sent a postcard from the airport to the man in Massachusetts who was driving me crazy: *Going to Israel.* I wanted to be unreachable, but I also wanted to feel safe.

I did. Safe, and absent. Everything in Israel seemed simpler, reduced to fundamentals: heat, sun, dust, crowds, Hebrew, surcease.

I had gotten off at the wrong bus stop for this kibbutz and had to walk miles along a featureless dusty road until an army officer gave me a lift. On my hike, I was exhilarated by the thought that there was no one in the world who knew where I was. I had truly escaped.

After dinner on my second night, Roberto asked me again if I felt like a moonlit walk as we left the large high-raftered dining hall. We passed the charming members' area where each balconied little building was fronted by a luxuriant garden. Below and beyond the crescent slope spread the sea, folding over its own darkness.

Roberto pointed at the full moon and I looked up.

"Well *I* will take a walk, then," he said, moving away to a patch that led down and down again to the beach, his yellow T-shirt and skimpy white shorts vivid against the night. I trailed back to my cot. The room stank of damp and darkness, and, lying down, I could only picture him barefoot on the sand.

I got up, took my key to lock the door behind me, and headed down the nearest path to the beach, slowly. Far up the coast the lights of Haifa broke in vivid steps down to the sea. I walked out across the gray-beige ripples of cool sand, each slap of water on the shore reminding me of home beyond the blue-black void, reminding me of far too much. . . .

Roberto waved and I moved down the beach.

"Why are you so sad?" he asked, his accent making the ordinary words warmer, caressive.

I turned, bent over to pull off my sandals, the *tanachniot* I had bought in Old Jaffa. We walked, and with only a few sentences from each of us, all the veils were lifted.

"We could be together," he said, pointing to some bushy-covered dunes down the beach. His accent, his swarthy sexiness, the moonlight made the line seem amazing. We headed in the direction of the two sand dunes that rose like a dull parenthesis waiting to be filled with meaning, information.

An army base lay some miles down the coast, and now the night was ground up by the roar of a jeep tearing through the sand and then fading, its radio crackling like gravel in a can.

On that trip in 1978, my first visit to Israel, I was barely skimming the surface of a country that was quite unreal to me, but deeply moving. It represented a path my parents hadn't taken. After liberation from their concentration camps, they lived in Belgium for several years, then emigrated to the United States, while my mother's surviving brother, Wolf, had headed for Israel as soon as he could. Uncle Wolf and his family sent pictures and occasional letters to us in New York. All of them looked dark and mysterious, especially my gorgeous cousin Asher and his older sister Shoshanah. But Israel to me had always seemed a half-formed fantasy despite the reality of their jobs, their home, their military service.

Although I was overwhelmed now by being in a Jewish country, bathing in it, I had very little contact and conversation with Israelis besides my aunt, uncle, and cousin Asher—and that was usually about American or Israeli politics. With nothing but infant Hebrew (it was my eight years of French that helped me the few times I got lost), I was isolated on my little island, hoping to see the sails of an English speaker approaching to rescue me. One evening I was at a wedding surrounded by people who didn't or wouldn't speak English. I can't remember now how I got there, but I remember the chilling fear and isolation amid the excitement, the food, the dancing. I belonged—after all, Israel was my country if I wanted it to be—but I was unutterably foreign.

Back then, I had no real sense of myself as a gay man, so the idea of even trying to find lesbians and gay men in Israel never even occurred to me.

II

After talking with lesbian and gay American Jews who have lived and traveled extensively in Israel over the last fifteen years, I understand that I might not have found much gay life even *with* a knowledge of Hebrew. Back in the late seventies, gays in Israel were fairly invisible. "It was like the Chinese and Cubans saying, 'We don't have them here,'" American social worker Ron Ben-Ezra notes with a laugh. "Israelis thought it just didn't exist. They thought it was something European, or American."

Even today, with increased media attention in Israel to gay issues, gay life is far more low-key and closeted than in the United States. At first glance, there may not be quite as many physical identifiers as there are in the United States, since Israel is such a homogeneous society. Almost everyone has shared the experience of being in the military, for instance, and despite the various national origins or backgrounds, the majority of Israel's population is Jewish. San Diego restaurateur Alan Bilmes finds that, in Israel, "People tend to fall into place rather than do things differently." Most Israelis want to be mainstream, according to Ben-Ezra, who spent eight years in Israel.

But more significant than whether you can tell who's gay and who isn't, what you won't find in Israel is the vast panoply of bars, restaurants, clubs, saunas, bookstores, resorts, the gay music and entertainment—all the things American gays and lesbians take for granted, at least as a possibility. This absence of what we would consider a rich gay subculture is just one element of Israeli gay life, a life that may be hard for American gays to imagine, and one in which, paradoxically, disadvantages offer some promise.

Israel is a tiny country lacking in privacy. About the size of New Jersey or Connecticut, Israel is home to fewer than five million people. If you're gay or lesbian, you don't have the options that American gays do. It's not like growing up in the Midwest and moving to San Francisco or New York to come out, build a new life, and abandon everyone you knew who might not want to accept you. In Israel, that kind of separation from family and home just isn't possible. You can't re-create yourself like Gatsby. Many families are a lot tighter and more tolerant, "because they have to be," says Barbara Baum, a Pittsburgh Jewish community worker who spent fourteen years in Israel. "They can't make up stories about their children to pass off to neighbors, because the children are around or not far away."

Galia Goodman, an artist in Durham, North Carolina, spent

about a year in Israel in the late eighties studying Hebrew and thinking about emigrating. She says that in Israel, "You can't escape the people who know the people you know. They're *everywhere*. You'll meet someone new who'll already have heard about you from a friend or a relative."

Baum said she found a remarkably "open" society. "The windows are always open," she recalls. "It's hard to have secrets."

Roger Kaplan recalls the day when he realized how very small a country Israel was. A Hebrew professor at Ohio State University, Kaplan has been to Israel more than half a dozen times since 1979. He recalls being on a hiking trip in the Golan Heights with his boyfriend, Uri. At least half an hour away from any town, they suddenly heard someone call "Hi!" Uri had run into his sister's ex-boyfriend from Tel Aviv.

While the ex-boyfriend did not assume that Roger and Uri were gay, Kaplan understood how hard it was to be gay in Israel. He also realized that if you're seen with someone who's known to be gay, there's "guilt by association." Most gays are so closeted you find that some don't use their full names when they sign letters in *Maga'im* (Contacts), one of the two gay magazines in Israel.

Feminist poet and historian Alice Young has spent time studying in Israel and working in the Israeli and Palestinian women's movement. Young observes that while Israeli lesbians may be aware of what they lack because the country is so small, Israel's size is "an advantage for an outsider." The lesbian community in Jerusalem is "tight and well organized," with regular meetings that are social and political.

Not only is Israel a small country, but "Israelis are nosy," says Bilmes, who travels to Israel at least once a year and has a wide network of friends there. "Israelis are blunt; they have no tact," says Baum. She had no intention of coming out there, but "they'll just ask you right out, or ask the person you buy eggs from. And he'll probably know!"

While more gays and lesbians are coming out, gay life to a large degree is still made up of cruising in public parks (for men), or meeting other lesbians and gays at private parties in people's homes. But even the privacy of someone's home is no protection against fear generated by being closeted. Goodman recalls, "I didn't meet anyone who was so open they felt comfortable with people being completely out." Goodman remembers women at parties walking into another room when someone showed up who was too politically active for them.

"They haven't grown up with positive gay role models," Kaplan observes. "So of course they're threatened by anyone who's out there." Ron Ben-Ezra was deeply involved in the growing politicization of Israeli gays, the move to decriminalize sodomy, and the legislation to end job discrimination against gays. As satisfying as that work was, he found that his political activity made it difficult to find and keep a lover.

Because Israel is so small and such a close-knit society, and because it's predominantly Jewish, there is tremendous cultural and social emphasis on family. "Noah's ark is real there," says Galia Goodman. "There's virtually no place for singles, gay or straight. Single women are perceived to be unhappy and there's tremendous pressure to be married. So gay friends tried setting me up with women, and straight friends who didn't know I was gay tried setting me up with men!"

Alan Bilmes recalls many supposedly straight married men cruising him on the street or trying to pick him up at parties. "It's no little land of virtue. And there's much more denial there than in the U.S." Goodman agrees. Women who are straight in Israel would most likely be lesbian in America, but they have husbands and children and are part of the community. "And if you come to Israel wondering if you're bisexual, there's so much emphasis on couples and marriage that you act out heterosexually." Goodman recalls conversations with other American Jewish lesbians who agreed that if for some reason they ended up stuck in Israel, they could see themselves getting married.

It is important to note that this emphasis on family life isn't identical with the right-wing Christian touting of family values so prevalent in the United States "Religion does shape attitudes in Israel," Kaplan finds, and Jerusalem may be fairly religious, but the country as a whole is not. Even though there are religious political parties that wield power in the government, homosexuality just isn't a significant issue for them. Those parties are far more interested in questions of religious education, stopping the desecration of burial sites, and the issue of territory. But there may also be an element of denial at work, Kaplan admits. Some Israelis might still want to insist that "Jews aren't homosexuals," so there's nothing to talk about.

Goodman is distressed by the impact of Israel's religious parties. "The Orthodox community has the country in a stranglehold.

There's no separation of church and state, no civil marriage, which means there'll never be gay marriage." In more general terms, she sees the religious influence as undergirding the widespread assumption that everyone in Israel is straight. "It's irritating to feel so invisible there."

"For many Israelis," Bilmes says, "homosexuality is a non-issue. They may have strong personal opinions, but basically they see it as a question of privacy that's not their business." Barbara Baum thinks that Israeli bluntness is actually a good thing in some ways. "They'll blurt out things that people here [in the U.S.] only think. No one's playing games there or trying to be politically correct. You might come out to someone who says, 'You're disgusting,' then later asks you some questions about being gay, and comes to accept it more quickly because they're not *trying* so hard to be understanding."

Ron Ben-Ezra recalls that around eighty percent of the Israelis urged to sign petitions about ending employment-related discrimination agreed that it was not fair, irrespective of whether they thought homosexuality was moral or immoral. Most surprising to him was that it was not possible to predict who would sign a petition based on class, background, or age. "All those stereotypes went out the window for me. Even Orthodox Israelis signed."

But he and Alice Young both agree that the antigay stereotypes in Israel are identical with those in the United States: Gay men are seen as effeminate, recruiting, child molesters; lesbians as "mannish" and man-hating. Ben-Ezra has heard an interesting twist on the stereotypes about the causes of homosexuality. Apparently some in the Hasidic community believe that if a woman thinks lascivious thoughts while conceiving, her son will be a homosexual!

In some ways, the fact that homosexuality is not a burning political or social issue may work to the benefit of lesbians and gays in Israel. As Jews, they are very well integrated and that may be one reason homophobia does not seem as powerful and pervasive a social force as in the United States Galia Goodman says she never felt physically threatened there as a lesbian. Ben-Ezra not only felt safe enough there to be physically affectionate in public, but safer than in New York, though he notes the increasing incidence of gay bashing as Israeli society has become more violent. On the other hand, Alice Young notes a surge in domestic violence and recalls how menaced she felt as a woman on her first trip to Israel in 1971. She was threatened by a soldier who followed her home from the beach. While she believes that it's still generally unsafe for women in a militarized society, she feels "totally safe" now with a solid base of lesbian friends and colleagues. But Barbara Baum says that straight and lesbian women face constant harassment in Israel.

Ben-Ezra, Young, and Baum have all been involved with recent political developments as Israeli lesbians and gays have become more public.

Ben-Ezra has seen a major revolution in gay visibility and awareness in the last ten years. A member of the Society for the Protection of Personal Rights (SPPR), and its political arm, Otzma (Power), he has seen the group's board become increasingly feminist and activist in tone, where it was once primarily social in focus. Initially, it was hard to get media coverage for its activities, but recently gay people and gay issues are much more visible in the Israeli press. That is partly due to what Ben-Ezra calls "a new generation of reporters" who are more open. He remembers a story about gay cops in Tel Aviv being fired becoming a news sensation in 1991, with reporters "baying" for information from the SPPR. A recent Gay Pride–related press conference got what Ben-Ezra called "serious attention and intelligent press," and a gay film festival had sellout crowds.

Other broader social changes have affected gay life in Israel, Ben-Ezra believes. Over the last ten years, Israelis have grown richer, have traveled more, and their increased exposure to European and American attitudes have made Israel more cosmopolitan. Anxieties about AIDS have also made Israeli society more aware, and sharpened the focus on gay concerns. Israel's HIV-positive rate is reported to be .2 percent per 1,000, but there's been a steady upsurge in HIV screening among all groups in the country's seven AIDS clinics, according to the *Detroit Jewish News*.

"Women in Black" is one of the first groups in Israel to urge the country's leaders to give up the West Bank and Gaza, using public demonstrations to raise consciousness. Alice Young notes that lesbians have played a major role in the group and in the Israeli women's movement in general. Young sees hope and excitement in the growing contacts developing between Israeli and Palestinian women. And her "uplifting" work with women makes her feel "hopeful and happy." Barbara Baum, also part of Women in Black, feels very positive about recent developments. "There really is a gay culture in Israel, and in Tel Aviv, gays almost seem to predominate."

Roger Kaplan is not so sanguine. Despite the changes, he detects a "strain of pessimism in Israeli gay men, who don't understand about achieving gay power, and even feel you have to look for a non-Israeli lover to be happy. It's a pre-Stonewall consciousness."

Israeli gays and lesbians have overcome some major legal obstacles that still face American gays, and Israel's Prime Minister Yitzhak Rabin, a former army chief of staff, says without equivocation that there is no reason to discriminate against gays in the military. Yet that discrimination continues, albeit inconsistently. Some people lose security clearance or don't get promoted as quickly as they might if they were straight, although Ron Ben-Ezra claims that it's widely known in Israel that much of military intelligence is gay.

Israelis leaving the country get more information about AIDS, which is still seen to be a foreign problem, than those already there. Tel Aviv now has a gay community center, but Bilmes sadly notes that it's underused. Yet over one hundred gays and lesbians met with ten Knesset members at the Knesset in February 1993 under the auspices of MK Yael Dayan, creating a media sensation.

Barbara Baum firmly believes that Israelis are becoming more tolerant and more aware. She cites as one example a class at Tel Aviv University's family counseling program: a required course in counseling gay couples. And because Israelis are more politically involved as a culture, there's hope for gays and lesbians as they become more open and political. Given how small Israel is, they're likely to see and feel the results of their efforts in ways American lesbians and gays cannot. The windows may be all that are wide open now, but the closet doors will surely follow.

III

So what happened with Roberto at the kibbutz? The sex was mostly exciting, but our few days together proved to be a disappointment. He was as deeply closeted as I was, so that it was impossible for us to talk about what we wanted from each other, or how we felt. At one midnight campfire on the beach, he freaked out when I reached for his hand in front of the other volunteers. I ended up fleeing the kibbutz just like I'd fled the United States.

I'm not remotely like that now. The next time I go to Israel, it will be with my Jewish partner of ten years. Gersh and I are supporters of the SPPR and we donated money for Tel Aviv's gay community center. Friends have promised to put us in touch with gay men and lesbians there and we hope to explore gay life with as much passion as we'll explore the country itself. I want to show him Masada, and Old Jaffa, and walk on that kibbutz beach, admiring the lights of Haifa. Maybe there'll be a moon. . . .

Losing My Mother

Today, my mother is in ruins, the blurred outline of a person. Rigid, eyes vacant, leaning sideways in a wheelchair, almost bald, eyes rheumy, she has to be fed. It takes my father two hours to get the food inside her unavailing mouth.

My brother holds her nose to force her mouth open. His way, she's fed in half an hour, forty minutes, tops. My father can't do it like that.

Face collapsed, she recognizes no one, and is silent. It is a vast and horrible silence that she fell into after strange leave-takings. When the small strokes became more severe and crippling, when she had to be put—at seventy-three—on drugs to keep her from violence, she spoke with a foreign gentleness, like a kindly scientist explaining very complicated processes to children barely able to comprehend. Her voice so soft you had to lean in. What was she saying?

My father, shaking his head, but listening, listening, said, "Nonsense." And when I listened, I heard amid the Russian of her childhood what sounded like rhymes, wordplay of some kind.

"She's not saying anything," my father insisted.

I thought she was saying good-bye. Retreating first from English and even her everyday Yiddish with my father, back into her first language, what she spoke in St. Petersburg until

1919 or 1920, and in Vilno afterward, retreating into Russian baby talk.

The baby talk was almost the end. After that, the sentences dried up, halted, seeming to collide with an invisible barrier. Perhaps they were simply tired—the burden of carrying so much of a life, its beginning and its end, too much, too crippling.

Finally, silence, at first broken by an intermittent "yes" or "no" when my father asked if she recognized him, recognized anyone.

He was trying to lure her back into life through speech. The last full sentence I ever heard from her was "Oh, Alex, stop bothering me!"—in English—after he asked her three times if she knew who I was. He would not admit that she was vanishing; regarded the slightest change, the slightest flicker of attention as proof that she would get better.

Even now, when she's been institutionalized for more than a year, he can insist, "She knows everything I say." And he is excited and convinced that on some days she's better.

But then he had denied her illness, covered it, for at least a year before she was institutionalized.

I suspected something. When I called home, she sounded tired, distracted. He almost always answered the phone. Hoping in my own blind way for change in our relationship, I thought he might be wanting more closeness between us. I thought he *wanted* to talk to me.

He knew something was wrong with her, so he kept her from the phone.

And I was a little relieved not to talk to her. She had been an unstoppable talker all my life. Sometimes unbearable. Once I had a friend over and I was in agony to get my mother to shut up, to leave us alone, to stop being so engaging, so loquacious. I couldn't believe she was so out of touch with the moment. Painfully gauche.

Her charm was too desperate. She had a heavy laugh that strained her throat—an attempt at lightness that wasn't easy for her, and not just because of the chain smoking, and her dark, persistent cynicism.

She was witty, probing, inexhaustible, talking as if to fend off silence, questions, doubts, pain, examination. Politics, in endless ramifications. She devoured the *New York Times* and played it back even if you had read the identical article. She talked about literature, too. Especially in her sixties when she went back to college, studied comparative literature, and adored Derrida, Lacan, the most incomprehensible writers. How could you even call their work "writing"? It was mud thrown at a screen. Yet she dug through the mud, delighted, talking, talking, practically a straight-A student. For Mother's Day during the years she went to school I could send her—along with flowers—something like a volume of poststructuralist film criticism and she would be *delighted.*

Perhaps it was the same impulse that made her do puzzles, acrostics, and read mysteries: a drive to finish something, to make order and sense.

My brother says one day, "Don't come in and see her. It's too depressing."

I say I'll fly to New York if she's dying, but to me, she's already dead and even in my dreams, she has nothing left to say.

The deconstructionists my mother reveled in sometimes print words *sous rature* ("under erasure"): with lines running through them to highlight the inadequacy of those words. The word is there/the word is struck out. Living and dead at the same time.

This year, in Israel, my uncle tells me the barest details of a story about her years in concentration camps that I had never heard before. Once, in a Latvian camp, she felt someone was punished for something she inadvertently said, and she tried to kill herself.

A German doctor saved her life.

The Holocaust swallowed her family, her home, her youth. Silence now has swallowed her past.

My brother says another day, "Maybe if you came in, she'd recognize you."

There is no magic to bring her back to life, to words.

My mother is under erasure.

Stories . . .

My mother had survived.

She had a striped concentration camp dress. She had a wooden ring with a number on it, but I didn't know where she had worn either. She never told me. She told me too little/too much.

When I was young, when I was not so young, when I was a

teenager and even in college, we sat in the L-shaped kitchen. A grim, ordinary Washington Heights Depression-era kitchen with a view of a gray side street out across a gated airshaft. We sat at the table that I saw years later in the window of a Los Angeles fifties kitsch shop: curving aluminum legs, ribbed aluminum sides topped by gray-patterned Formica, the poor man's marble. The table in LA was lit as if it were a Merovingian relic. But where was my mother to make it real?

We sat and drank coffee and talked about school and life and books and whatever. But there was always another presence there at the table in that quiet room: the haunted, haunting past. The past that emerged in stories, or bits of stories. Maybe just flashes. These stories slipped into my life, like an unseen cat that suddenly springs to slash your hand.

They didn't happen to me, but they're mine, now, or at least what I can remember of them. And so they live inside me, making me—sometimes—afraid of crowds. The panic I have felt in a football stadium after a game as hordes surge down the ramps, and I am swept along, powerless to pull myself away or out, powerless to stop. Feeling I want to scream so they'll let me go.

Flashes.

—*"In ghetto"* (those words were in Yiddish), "we ground up glass and wrapped it with a little food to put in the rat holes, then stuffed the holes with whatever we could find." I think I was supposed to admire her cleverness. The resourceful Jews trapped by the Nazis, taking care of themselves. All I could think of was the rats, coming through the walls, my walls.

—"A Polish woman said to me, You can always tell a Jew. They have such sad eyes."

—"When they liquidated the ghetto, Polish women spit on us as we were marched out."

But here I have to stop. How old was I when those words became not just part of my vocabulary, but part of my life? Liquidated. Ghetto. This is not the imagination of disaster, this *is* disaster. I will never not know these words or foggy images. I will never escape.

—"They shaved our heads." Here, she breaks off, and the words float in my memory like a ragged cloud, with only empty sky around it. She rarely said even those four words together. But years later, I think they hide behind a different pain. When my mother starts losing her hair, the hair that was luxuriant, alive— before the War, and even after for some years. She suffers new defeats. In all of New York, she can't find a wig that looks good. But then, what wig can hide the losses no one sees? She tries some vitamins, and wisps of hair grow back, but cannot hide her higher brow. I suggest a different man to cut and style and dye her hair, but she erupts in tears, pleading to be let alone: "There is no hair there!"

It's hopeless is what she means, but I press and press, wanting her to hope, just a little, just about her hair, her looks, something. She was so beautiful once, and now she's given up. Or so it seems to me, a boy who hasn't lived in hell.

Gas

I came to dread the ringing of the phone. Because of times like this—times before I knew how sick my mother was:

Casually, my brother Sam tells me, "Mom isn't going out as much. She has gas."

This is not a conversation I want to have. Yet I cannot help asking, "Gas? Why? What's wrong?"

"It's her ulcer medication, I think."

"Can't they give her something for the gas?" But even I know that she probably hasn't mentioned it to her doctor. Embarrassment. "And what about shopping?"

"Dad does it."

I don't know what to say. I'm appalled to talk about my mother's gas. Partly, it's the word itself. Farting is a different word, a different world—farting is funny, farting is Chaucer. And for me, a writer, it's distance. The Age of Farts: a literary epoch in which farting is a part of life, something you can write about with joy.

But gas is something else. Gas is death. It has been a dirty word for me as long as I can remember. Gas killed my mother's mother, and countless other Jews.

Desperate to quell the moles creating their condos in my gorgeous back yard, I hesitantly buy gas shaped like sticks of dynamite. Poison pellets haven't worked, and the thought of steel and crushing traps disgusts me. Gas is all that's left.

I'm in the gardening aisle of a local supermart. Boxes and bottles promising death to pests face bottles and boxes trumpeting growth and blooms. I lurk like someone in an adult bookstore afraid of being recognized. I make my shoddy purchase and tell no one how ashamed I am to gas even unseen life. But I feel like a murderer anyway. And then, I'm slightly relieved, because the gas has no effect except to drive *me* from the yard.

My mother's gas. No end to cruelty. The ghetto, the starvation, the camps. And now my mother once again is trapped. By gas. Like Mrs. Mendelssohn, my piano teacher for eight years. Rose Mendelssohn, a Russian Jew. Frail, slim, dithering, in her seventies, one day at our lesson, she has gas. Shocked, sixteen or so, I sit there as she plays some frantic chords to drown the crescendo of stuttering from inside herself. As if it weren't there. Banging out those chords. Crescendo. Hiss. She says nothing. I say nothing. But soon I understand that this is why her lessons have dried up. I know this is why her apartment in our building has a strange metallic smell.

It isn't long before she stops her lessons, or they stop her, and I have no more interest in the piano anyway. It isn't long before she's locked inside her apartment and the super's wife stands outside the black steel-clad door, calling, "Rosie, Rosie, come out." Like a children's game. Finally, the woman phones one of Mrs. Mendelssohn's daughters. They take her "away."

All this happens offstage. I hear it from my mother, who sneers at Mrs. Mendelssohn's rich children. Children off in some suburb, who rarely descend from their heights to our deteriorating Washington Heights, children who have abandoned their mother (so my mother says). Abandoned her to a stale apartment where she doesn't wash or clean or eat, but broods or drifts, a gentle wraith.

"I don't want to end up like that," my mother says. Over and over. This is her greatest fear, greater than expecting cancer, which she does whenever she is weak or ill.

My mother's aunt also wound up "like that," sliding into oblivion, knowing nothing in her eighties but regrets and accusations.

I remember reading of the camps, of gas, of Nazi gas. And more: the Jews, their guts betrayed by lack of food, betraying. Everything stripped away, including dignity. Especially dignity.

On some slave labor crew digging, hauling rocks, my mother says a man called out "Hey you!" to a German Jew, who reared up. "I am Herr Doktor Professor Schmidt—not 'hey you!'"

"You're just a stinking Jew like all the rest of us," is the reply. And yes, they stink. No wonder my mother was always fastidious, talked and nagged at home about "hygiene."

How has she come to this? Once elegant, battered now by time, bursting inside, drawing inward from the world. It mortifies me to think of her reduced to helplessness.

And, most horribly, I recall the last time I was home, how she didn't know I was awake—I think—and there was a thunderclap of gas beyond belief when she awoke and made her bed.

I tell none of this to Sam.

Smoking

"Tiny white spots on the brain," my father repeats.

I have asked him what the doctor said, what the MRI showed, what it all means, what the name is, hoping to find power in a word or words. He can't remember.

I ask again. Exasperated, my father says, "What do I know what it's called? It's tiny white spots on the brain—I saw the picture."

"But that's not the name of an illness—that's . . ."

Well, what is it?

Like those brutal black and white photos of bombed Iraq. I see the territory of her brain laid waste. Not so long before, I had been haunted by air raid sirens on the nightly news—in Israel, Saudi Arabia, and Iraq. I imagined the terror of waiting for bombs to strike, the noise, the concussion, the stench, the utter powerlessness. It was impossible for me to hear the sirens and not picture my mother and her parents trapped at a funeral in a hurricane of German bombs in 1941, or my father—a slave laborer for the Hungarian army—digging trenches under constant bombardment by the Soviets.

How is there so much violence in her brain?

I'm driving from LaGuardia airport with my father to see why my mother is locking herself out of the apartment, losing her keys, waiting for him downstairs hours before he's due to come home.

"Mom called me to ask what every four hours means," my brother has said. "For one of her prescriptions." This prompted my flight from Michigan. My alarm turns to despair when my father and I misconnect at the airport and we look for each other for half an hour. I call their home and my mother drowsily repeats, "He went to the airport to pick up the man who is arriving."

She doesn't know who I am right now, she's confused, can't take a message, can't follow what I try to tell her.

It's worse than I thought. A series of small strokes has ripped apart the woman she was. Now my father keeps asking, "You think it's bad?" after telling me each new horror in the car, after lamenting, "The poor girl—the poor girl. How can this happen to her?"

I want to scream at him. I want to make him drive like the young man he is not, instead of letting his right foot ease on and off the gas pedal as if he sat at a sewing machine. I want to flee whatever is ahead.

"Such a sickness, it never was in my family," my father says.

"Strokes can be caused by smoking. It's probably all the smoking," I say. "That's not hereditary. Two packs a day—"

"No. Mother never smoked like that."

"Two packs a day!"

Furious, he denies it. But I know two is close to the truth. I used to run out and buy her Larks for her. We wrangle. But it must be true.

Like dogs growling over a blanket tugged tight between them, we go back and forth about her smoking. I begin to wonder if he's right.

The next day I relay this conversation to my brother, who smiles as if my father's denial of reality is nothing new.

"But she did smoke a lot, didn't she?" I'm begging to be believed.

"All the time," Sam says, though that's no longer our concern.

Just to be sure, that weekend I call my oldest friend to check. Thankfully she says, "Lev, I never saw your mother *without* a cigarette. She was a chain smoker. Really."

But why did I badger my father? What difference did it make what caused the nightmare in her brain, the cave-in, the collapse? Why can't we grieve together?

I am blaming him, my mother, me.

The bombs have hit us all and left us dazed amid the smoking ruins.

Names

Names are nothing constant in a life. My father's name is Alex now but never was for years. He was born as Shlomo. Solomon. A name with history and grandeur (unlike the nickname Shloimy), connected to the Jewish past. But in a time when Nazis and their friends destroyed the Jewish present, past, and future, burning people, books, and towns, his name was lost.

Captured by Hungarians, he became Szandor. Like a flooded valley where the towns lie ghostly underneath the brand new lake, he was Shloimy still. And underneath there was more. He was descended from the Temple priests, a Levi, and then so was I.

But he was nothing much to the Hungarians. He never was a man, he's just a Jew.

They used him as a tool, dragged him with the other slaves on their way to fight the Soviets. He dug trenches in the winter blasts, his shovel striking sparks on frozen ground.

But he survived. Survived the guard who threw a hand grenade at him but killed his friend. My father sports the shrapnel in his legs—a lasting gift. His friend's head disappeared in chunks.

And he survived his flight, his hiding with a priest who taught him Latin prayers to masquerade. Recounting this, he cried. Stolen name and stolen faith. Another flight and he was captured, finally, in Budapest or Prague (which one, which one?), and shipped to Bergen-Belsen, where a German pointed a gun at his head and asked his name. He didn't fire, smiling: they had the same last name.

I learned all this in his isolated moments of recall. He would start speaking as if overcome, a medium in touch with worlds beyond, and questions would have stopped the flow, so I said nothing, just brought him schnapps to down.

Somewhere in these scraps of narrative I learned he faced an execution once, or did my mother tell me that? Faced a firing squad, but British bombers overhead delayed his death.

And I learned he fought guerrilla war, sharpshooting from some hills. I only knew this when he read a movie sign from blocks away, amazing me. "That's nothing. I could shoot a Nazi from much farther away."

In his accent *farther* sounded like *fodder*. Which he was.

And afterward in postwar time, marooned in Brussels, Szandor made a Belgian Alexandre, shortened on his Brussels documents to Aleks.

My mother's name also suffered transformation. Born in Petrograd, she was Lia Helena. Lia disappeared in Poland, I don't know why, and living with my father for five years in Brussels once they were free, her name was Hélène.

But Americans couldn't stand the foreignness in 1950, and it was bleached away to dowdy Helen, stripped of euphony and grace.

There was a deeper loss. My father's family name, Steinberg, was not his own, or not for long. It was the imposition of an eighteenth-century Austrian law that Jews should have real (German) names. "Stein" means stone and "berg" means mountain—an empty, brutish German name.

No wonder Sam, my brother, wants to change his name. Born in Brussels, he is only Sam, there's no trace of French about him. He'd like to be "Alain," at least to add it onto Sam—a middle name where he has none.

"Why not?" I say, but something holds him back.

Not me. Twice, I've named myself. Once to wrestle free, to be myself. I chose my uncle's name, the one who died at Stalingrad. And Lev meant many things. Heart in Hebrew. Lion in Yiddish. Two pieces of my life.

And then again, five years along, I dropped my father's name and chose one that means "God will heal" to mark my new connection to my faith.

I escaped the German branding iron, decolonized myself.

Came down from my father's mountain, as, I think, my brother can't or won't.

Lines

It wasn't a bedtime story. Nothing to make me sleep. It was a nightmare. My mother in one line, her mother in the other. The line going to the right: to gas, to death, to flames.

Is it any wonder my mother was obsessed for years with asking if the stove is off? Leaving the apartment, driving off, she'll say, "Alex? Did I turn off the stove?" What is her vision? Gas and flames ripping apart the life she has, the life she rescued from the past?

I do it, too. Older now, perhaps as old as she was when I first noticed her concern. I ask Gersh, Did you check the stove? Sometimes he laughs; sometimes I dread that passenger inside, that memory of her in fear.

It's an electric stove, but still I can see myself driving back to find our home a black and ugly pile, destroyed. The quiet tree-lined street scarred by smoke and stink. My secret terrors. Like hearing noises late at night and imagining a murderer, a gun or many knives. I know from my own parents' past that nothing is ever safe. Most of the time, it is knowledge I suppress.

Those fatal lines. Was that the same scene, the same camp where an elegant woman opened a casket of jewels for the Nazi officer in charge to beg for freedom, or at least for life? You can imagine what she got, my mother adds, and I don't ask.

Torn apart. From home, from friends, from family, from life. I worry when Gersh is late, or doesn't call when he said he would. I fear an accident, his death.

My brother says he heard a different story about lines. My mother told him something else. That her mother understood the meaning of the lines at once, shoved my mother across to life, to hope, despite her cries. Someone beat them both and that was all. My mother lived. Knowing she was saved by her own mother's hands.

Who could live with such a scene? And yet she did. Maybe that's the scene that came back when my mother's brain caught fire, when she attacked my brother, my father too, threw plants across the room, and shouted out in German.

I couldn't bear to ask for more, to ask what words returned to her, what pain. Knowing they were German was bad enough. I have rarely heard her speak that poisoned tongue.

I wonder why she told us different versions of the truth. Was there some lesson we should learn? Did Sam know more because he's older, because he heard it closer to the past? As she grew older, was that crucial shove too much to think about, repeat?

Who would *I* save knowing that it meant my life?

Castles

Books made great walls. Before I learned how to read, I would drag my brother's hardback books from the three-shelved beige book-case at one end of our large open room, scooch down by the big cardboard box full of toys, and proceed to build a "castle." Cross-legged and happy on the gray-, red-, and black-flecked linoleum, chattering to myself, I'd stand the books on end, creating square keeps with massive double doors that could either slide or swing open. I wasn't concerned with scale, except to try to make the books fairly even in height. The smooth, shiny covers, usually monochrome, made the walls seem resolute and unscalable.

The big fat books were the most satisfying, like one about bees and ants, with a glossy maroon cover.

Plastic figures of all kinds—animals, men, it didn't matter—would march along the tops as if behind thick battlements, taunting their enemies, protecting themselves, surveying their domain. These were not the elegant, pennoned castles of my cutout books, where each brick looked as real as the artist could make it. And though I could use the cutout knights on my book battlements, they bent or tore and were only two-dimensional, while my own castles had three dimensions, if not more.

My book castles didn't have the solidity and grace of the ones I could make using the light brown blocks we kept in a cloth bag, blocks that clattered against each other when I lifted the bag from my toy box. There were some triangles and arches among the blocks, and along with the squares and rectangles, I could use these to simulate towers and doorways in a castle that wasn't likely to tip over, as the books might. But the neutral-colored blocks weren't as exciting, unless I mixed them up in some way with the books.

The books were always more satisfying. The walls higher and thicker, guarding the secrets inside.

I wanted to be inside those walls, protected, safe.

There was too much anger outside those walls, too much shouting and pain.

I didn't know then that my parents had survived concentration camps, but I knew they had come from somewhere else, from Europe—a land of castles and knights in my imagining—and had somehow been imprisoned.

But they were still in prison.

And I picked up this fear, I played with it. Coming home from school, I'd imagine our building besieged. Some enemy was swarming in from the street. I held them off at the buzzer door, then from behind a barricade in the hall, always falling back, but always resilient. It was a mental tic, a game, a spell. Practicing destruction.

I used colored clays to build castles in the bathroom sink, whose walls I breached to see the water flow, and drown whatever was inside.

It was an easy game to play. I lived in a castle. Our building was on one of the many hills of Washington Heights. The dark wide lobby was gloomy, and picturesque with its sconces, carved tables, deep window embrasures, and touches of marble. Coming home, walking in off a fairly treeless stretch of Broadway, was like entering another era.

Our apartment was on the eighth floor, and one of the windows in the bedroom I shared with Sam was a double window with a glittering view of upper Manhattan, the Hudson River, the tree-thick Palisades, the sturdy, graceful George Washington Bridge, and the hilly, mysterious overgrown cemetery of downtown's Trinity Church. It was like being in a tower.

There were castles all around me. The local library, off 145th Street, near the Gothic-looking elementary school.

My notebooks were full of towers, castles. I liked the idea of being far away and enclosed.

The first thing I remember painting in school was a tower on a hill. The easel stood at the back of class, and I didn't have much time there. The paints ran. When I did any art project, the clumsiness of my hands undid me.

I was safer with my books.

Writing Something Real

All through college, my creative writing teacher kept predicting that I would be published someday, even win prizes, but not until I wrote something "real." I didn't know what she meant at the time, although I can see it now. I was writing comic sketches about working-class couples, and what I thought of as high English farce. I even attempted a gothic romance about a girl locked in a tower by her father, who played Beethoven in the gloomy parlor below while she lamented her fate and wrote tearful sonnets. I'd read one too many Victoria Holt novels, I guess.

My writing was as far away from myself as possible, and by that I mean as far away from my world, my own observations, my own truest knowledge. It was secondhand, drawn from other people's books.

Yet it was two classic novels I read in my senior year that first opened me up to my own depths, connected me to myself in such a way that I could never quite return to falseness and hiding—at least in my writing. Edith Wharton's *The House of Mirth* and Henry James's *The Portrait of a Lady* had a lasting impact on me by forcing me to begin confronting my own demons: the fear of being gay, and my unwillingness to claim a positive Jewish identity.

What was in these two books that kept me reading into the middle of the night, breathless, transfixed, aware of myself as utterly changed? Wharton's masterpiece is the story of a woman destroyed by a society that offers her one choice alone: marriage. There is no other way for Lily Bart to live the life she has been trained to expect as rightfully hers because she is beautiful, graceful, and gifted with impeccable taste. Perhaps the most crushing moment in the book takes place on the Riviera, when Lily is publicly and unmistakably branded as an adulteress. Soon after, she discovers that she is virtually disinherited by the aunt who has not too generously taken care of her since her parents' death, in part because of that scene. Twin humiliations: two moments in which Lily Bart is alone, stared at, the object of scorn and pity, and irrevocably cast out. Life's hopes and possibilities continually elude and defeat Lily.

James's heroine, Isabel Archer, is a free-spirited, optimistic, and challenging woman, whose huge inheritance leads her into a blind alley. In the novel's most poignant chapter, Isabel understands that the man she married, hoping to give herself a wider view of life, is really the exact opposite of what she expected. He is petty, mean, and shallow. She feels hopeless and trapped. So did I. Although I had known I was attracted to men from first grade on, I had never allowed myself to carry this attraction forward into anything more than furtive hugs and soppy poetry. Instead, I dated women, compelled by the dictates of a society that even in liberated 1970s New York hated homosexuals. I could not face the possibility of being scorned and cast out as Lily Bart had been.

I am a first-generation American. My first language, however, was Yiddish, not English.

When I started writing fiction in earnest in high school and college, it expressed my desire to erase my difference, to flee into another reality, any reality. My writing was profoundly un-Jewish, it said nothing about the Holocaust and ignored sexual conflict.

No wonder my fiction was full of disguises. It read like a series of desperate flares sent up for help.

My creative writing teacher in college understood those flares, and she was the first person I came out to.

I did it on the phone one evening, because I figured if it went badly I could always hang up.

"Kris," I said. "I have something to tell you."

"Do I need a drink to hear this?" I didn't catch the irony in her reply, just the warmth.

"Yes—a big one."

"Wait a minute—hold on—don't hang up!" I heard a cabinet door open, the clink of bottles, glassware, ice.

"I'm back."

Whispering now, unable to hang up, driven by the urge to tell someone and captured by the momentum of release, I said, "I have these feelings—" I couldn't go further, but she did, nonchalantly.

"Feelings about men?"

Her insight and lack of surprise made me laugh. And later I found out that two other students in the same class had come out to her, not long before. Also on the phone. But her ease wasn't mere practice or pedagogy, it was the natural expression of a nurturing wise woman whose gift was seeing potential in her student's potential of many kinds. I registered for every class she taught.

In her novel classes, I read authors who took me deeper into myself: Samuel Butler, Theodore Dreiser, Henry James, F. Scott Fitzgerald, George Eliot, Edith Wharton. In her writing workshops, she kept up the pressure on me to write something, anything, that was real. Yes, my medieval fantasies were amusing, but I was floating on the surface of the story. Every story. My own stories.

My senior-year conflicts about whether I should marry a non-Jewish girl, in combination with reading Wharton and James, finally propelled me into writing that was unmistakably more real, writing that dealt with characters' feelings as facts and not fantasies, writing that traveled into uncertainties of the heart and not mere plot complications, writing that didn't constantly pat itself on the back for being so clever. This new depth was unexpectedly aided by the theater courses I was taking. Not because I learned about myself in rehearsal and onstage, but because I had never before felt so tantalized and so completely an outsider. Never truly their equal or even their colleague, I was moved to write and observe the other students in this self-dramatizing, cliquish, mean-spirited department. I was suddenly a budding anthropologist, recording details of an alien world.

In my graduate writing program a year later, I was drawn to new discoveries, not all of them pleasant. I learned that the need for a man had been so stifled in me by internalized homophobia, by my own shame, that I could not only accept an unsatisfactory and even demeaning relationship but glory in it as if living an opera. Surely I deserved to feel tormented? But I also learned the joy of being with other writers, of taking myself seriously, and of being published in *Redbook* at twenty-four.

In Amherst, for the first time in my life I gave way completely to the admission that I wanted another man. This wasn't a fantasy, this was the provocative presence of someone in my dorm. I said the words—I wrote it down in my journal. He had dropped by my room one night to chat—a large, broad Viking of a man, easygoing, sensuous, relaxed. That week, I had been reading two novels of obsession: Susan Hill's eerie *The Bird of Night* and Emily Brontë's *Wuthering Heights*, and I was primed for an explosion of *some* kind. While Fred and I talked, suddenly I saw him with complete clarity at the same time that I knew I wanted him, desperately, with such force that the frenzy of my pulse made me wonder why every item in the room didn't burst apart.

The revelation devastated me afterward—I could feel a tremendous shift inside, and knew I was in the middle of a crisis in which the decision seemed to be: stop writing and hide, or keep writing and open up. To write at all, to write honestly, was to stir up everything inside of me that was painful and unresolved. I couldn't turn back.

So I wrote about the son of Holocaust survivors who felt alienated by his parents' past, and crushed by it. Writing that story, staying open, was a choice.

My writing workshop hated the story, and so did the professor.

It's very satisfying to report that two weeks later, Martha Foley, editor of *The Best American Short Stories*, awarded it the Harvey

Swados Prize. A year later, it was published in *Redbook*, which then had 4.5 million readers. I was being taken seriously as a writer, I was making money on my work.

But publishing in *Redbook* led me into typical New York blindness. Starting there, winning a prize—weren't those natural first steps of an easy ascent to cash and fame?

For five or six years after that, every story I sent to national magazines, and even the major literary quarterlies, was rejected. Opening the mailbox I felt assaulted by the manila envelopes— sometimes five in a day—defeated, crushed. It was my own misjudgment; I thought that everything I wrote was as good as my first publication. I thought the only place worth publishing was in a magazine like *Redbook*, or better. Moving to Michigan, I could slowly cut loose of those expectations and ask simple questions: What did I have to say in my writing? Who was my audience?

A story I wrote in one evening was the first to break the drought. It was accepted immediately by a Jewish magazine, and my stories began to appear in a widening range of Jewish publications. I became something of a Jewish celebrity in East Lansing (which I could imagine my father dismissing as a *knappeh metziah*—no big deal).

But feeling restored as a writer, hopeful again, and finally connected as a Jew, I was only halfway there. It wasn't until I fell in love with my partner, Gersh—who is Jewish—that I was able to begin bridging the two worlds. It was loving him and being loved (feeling safe) that gave me the courage to write my first gay *and* Jewish short story—an early version of the title piece of my collection

Dancing on Tisha B'Av. And when it was included in a national anthology of gay fiction a few years after being published in an obscure Jewish magazine, I suddenly had a new audience developing. Ultimately what brought me the most attention as a writer was adding another circle of readers by stepping out into a gay audience, but unmistakably as a Jew.

The epigraph for my first book, *Dancing on Tisha B'Av*, is from Don DeLillo's brilliant novel *Players*: "To speak it in words is to see the possibilities emerge." Speaking all across the United States, in Canada, Great Britain, France, and Germany, I have learned the truth of that line for myself and others. In Germany, touring with *Das Deutsche Geld* (*The German Money*), my first book to be translated into German, I was asked many questions at bookstores, schools, and institutes. Perhaps most striking was this one: "Can there be forgiveness?"

I wouldn't have been there, and wouldn't be writing, if the answer were no.

Letter from Israel, II

I once asked a friend who spent lots of time in Israel what gay life was like there and he ruefully said, "They have a pre-Stonewall consciousness."

But that was before May 30, 1994, when four screaming right-wing demonstrators interrupted a wreath-laying ceremony by gays and lesbians at Yad Vashem, Israel's Holocaust memorial and museum in Jerusalem. The resulting melee made news worldwide and thrust Israeli gays and lesbians to center stage in the Israeli media in a way they never expected (and some regret).

I was in Israel for two weeks with my partner, Gersh. We had started the day of the Yad Vashem ceremony in Jerusalem and visited the Western Wall on the first of four days of intensive touring around Israel before the conference. Our travels would also involve spending lots of time with Israeli gays.

The ceremony was the first and most solemn event of a week leading up to an Israeli and European conference of gay and lesbian Jews at Givat Haviva, a kibbutzlike conference center an hour or so north of Tel Aviv. Several days before May 30, a group of American rabbis had taken an ad in the *Jerusalem Post* decrying the planned ceremony and talking about gays in the blood-and-thunder language American gays are used to hearing from the religious right. The stage was thus set for some kind of confrontation at a spot that is sacred in many ways to Israelis and Jews everywhere. Foreign leaders visiting Israel invariably lay wreaths in Yad Vashem's Hall of Remembrance at the eternal flame, and various Jewish groups often do the same. This, however, was the first time that such an event was sponsored by Israel's gay and lesbian civil rights group, the Society for the Protection of Personal Rights (SPPR).

On May 30, 150 Israeli, European, and American gay Jews waited to say prayers in memory of gay and lesbian Jews who died in the Holocaust. Many were children of Holocaust survivors. We stood along the raised broad platforms forming two sides of the Hall of Remembrance, whose black granite floor bears the names of concentration camps that are seared into my family's history, and into the memory of the Jewish people—names like Majdanek, Bergen-Belsen, Auschwitz, Stutthof.

The short ceremony started with singing of the Song of the Vilno Ghetto Partisans and chanting of prayers, but it was almost immediately interrupted by a hysterical demonstrator who was later identified as a member of Israel's banned right-wing Kach party. He shrieked, tore his hair, and rolled on the ground, calling us "evil," saying we were "full of shit" and worse, accusing us of blasphemy, of desecrating the site. This same man claimed that his father had been murdered (some news stories said raped) by a homosexual Nazi camp guard.

The ceremony went on in the midst of chaos, as eager cameramen scurried like cockroaches after this man—and then another, and then two more—while Yad Vashem attendants and police tried to subdue and eject them.

Gersh and I were paralyzed. I wondered if this was what it was like during World War II in Europe—that is, seeing something so unbelievable that you were utterly unable to respond or know how to respond. Should I leave? Should I leap down from the platform onto the floor to make the demonstrators stop? I was amazed at the hatred I suddenly felt, wishing I could silence those monsters of intolerance.

The ceremony went on—even after someone snatched pages from the hand of the chanting gay rabbi. Some people shouted the words of the Kaddish (prayer for the dead) at the demonstrators to drown them out. Then we all locked arms and sung the poet and partisan Hannah Senesch's plangent and moving hymn "Eli, Eli." That was met by howling contempt: a demonstrator shouted that we were defiling her memory and her words because we were gay.

In half an hour, the ceremony and the uproar were over—or so I thought.

News coverage in the United States and even radio reports focused on the shouting and the apparent violence at Yad Vashem, but it missed the aftermath in Israel's media, which we were able to follow in detail along with our Israeli friends. Gays fared badly on Israeli TV, where the rhetoric on talk shows *starts* with the incendiary. But many Israeli newspapers strongly condemned the demonstrators' outrageous and ugly behavior. The speaker of the Knesset (who is a Holocaust survivor) accused them of "fascist" tactics in trying to silence their opponents and said that if some of these protestors were survivors themselves, they had learned nothing from their ordeal.

Most inspiring was the reaction of fiery Knesset member Yael Dayan, who made it very clear that this attack on gays was linked to other hatreds: of Arabs, of secular Jews, of women. Dayan wrote in *the Jerusalem Post* that "anyone who believed in [Israel's] future as an egalitarian, democratic, humane society, one which accepts those who are different and supports their rights as a minority, ought to wear a pink triangle, next to the yellow star and blue-and-white."

Dayan was also the keynote speaker at the SPPR-sponsored conference that started four days after the Yad Vashem ceremony, and she received a standing ovation there before she spoke a word. At Givat Haviva, Dayan's empathy and anger were unswerving. Speaking to an audience of nearly three hundred Israeli, European, and North and South American Jewish gays and lesbians, she made it very clear that those fanatics in Israel who hated gays, objected to peace, and also objected to human rights—these people suffered "an inability to understand or accept the Other." Dayan said to us, "Your hurt is my outrage; your tears give me voice and strength." Gersh and I felt empowered and uplifted, wishing that there were more American politicians who could speak out for gays so unambiguously.

Reactions to the Yad Vashem incident among Israeli gays were very mixed. Some were elated at their sudden high visibility and the appearance in print of allies. Others, like Israel's premier gay poet, Ilan Schoenfeld, were stunned by the negative press. Schoenfeld was in an unrivaled position to chart these reactions because he was the SPPR's publicist for the conference. "My fax and my phone didn't stop ringing for days," he told us over lunch at Cafe Nordau, Tel Aviv's charming and very popular gay restaurant. He was afraid that the hostility aroused by the fracas at Yad Vashem would backfire on Israel's gays.

Yet many of the gays and lesbians I spoke to felt inspired by facing their critics, which is somewhat new, because gays in Israel are very closeted.

I saw how intimate (and intrusive) Israel could be when our tour visited Masada the day after the Yad Vashem incident. In the jammed cable car coming back down from the mountain palace-fortress built by King Herod, a woman asked our tour guide (who was also gay) if we were "the group" that had been at Yad Vashem (was it because some of us were enjoying being shoved together?). Our guide said yes, and the two of them fell into an increasingly fiery discussion in Hebrew in which she—herself a tour guide—denounced us for upsetting Israel's three hundred thousand Holocaust survivors. She was also worried about who would get married if there were too many gays and lesbians, and said she hoped none of her children were gay.

One of the highlights of our wonderful two-week trip was attending the opening of a used bookstore-coffee shop in Jerusalem's historic and very beautiful Nahalat Shiva district, the first independent Jewish settlement outside the old city walls, established in the mid-nineteenth century. With a pedestrian mall, gorgeous stone buildings, and lively restaurants, it's the very image of a confident, economically powerful Israel. David Erlich, the store's owner, is a young Israeli gay writer.

Israel's Nobel prize-winning poet Yehuda Amichai read that evening, and it seemed that hundreds of people were in and out all night, many of them friends of ours from the conference. At one point, someone took Gersh up to the front of the store. "See those two shelves in that bookcase? That's the first gay section in any bookstore in Israel." Many people told me that they went to London or Amsterdam to buy gay and lesbian books. The paucity of gay literature may explain the success of one of David Leavitt's books when it was translated into Hebrew.

"It's very hard to be a gay writer here," Schoenfeld told us, as he described the pressure from publishers to tone down the gay content of his work, and the various projects and anthologies he'd like to do if he only had the time and the access. Schoenfeld talked movingly about the possibility of starting a small gay press, but it was clearly one of many dreams, especially because Schoenfeld's publicity work takes so much of his time.

As I did my reading at Givat Haviva during the SPPR-sponsored conference, I was keenly aware that there was no gay *Israeli* poet or fiction writer on the program. After the reading, an Israeli man came up to tell me that his fiction was becoming more homoerotic, but he felt stymied about where to publish it. There wasn't much specific help I could offer.

When I told a gay writer friend I was going to be reading in Israel, he said, "The homophobia must be terrible there." The extremely photogenic outbursts at Yad Vashem will no doubt confirm stereotypic views of Israeli society as deeply antigay, but the truth is much more complex, as I've described in my "Letter from Israel, I" (chapter 3).

And despite the theatricality and publicity of the outbursts at Yad Vashem, it's hard to believe that antigay rhetoric will ever become a driving force in Israel's political scene, as it is in the United States. An Israeli interviewer trying to get me and Gersh on a national radio show to talk about what happened at Yad Vashem wasn't concerned when our schedules didn't work out: "It's a big story now, but not for long."

Yet many of the Israelis discussing the incident at Tel Aviv's glossy new gay community center (which has a remarkably rich library of English-language gay titles) seemed to agree that "something like this had to happen." Gays and lesbians in Israel had to see the depth of the hatred in at least part of Israel's populace, had to see the worst facing them. "We're not babies anymore," I heard from several gay Israelis. More defiantly, more proudly, many said with a sense of discovery, "This is our Stonewall."

Selling Was Never My Line

As a shy, somewhat overweight, sexually confused teenager with bad teeth, I hated working at my father's little store in New York's Washington Heights. I felt exposed and embarrassed. I was bad at arithmetic and panicky at the cash register when people said things like, "I have a nickel." I had no idea what they meant.

I swore to myself that when I grew up, I would never do retail. But that's exactly what happened when I launched a book tour that led to over one hundred readings and signings promoting my collection *Dancing on Tisha B'Av* and my novel *Winter Eyes*. I've read at bookstores, synagogues, universities, Jewish community centers, and writers' conferences—from Pittsburgh to Paris.

Along the way, I've probably met (and forgotten the names of) more people while touring than I have met in my entire lifetime. I've completely overcome my feelings of "I don't get out enough." I've earned tens of thousands of frequent-flyer miles. I know the way to the Lansing airport in my sleep. I've gone deeply into debt and I feel as dazed and bedraggled as Agnes Gooch in *Auntie Mame* realizing that she's "lived."

It all started innocently enough at the 1990 Out/Write, the first national conference of lesbian and gay writers. I was blissfully floating in a sea of writers, publishers, editors, and journalists, and

meeting people I wanted to meet and some who wanted to meet me. I was enjoying the excitement of starting something new, of being part of a vibrant community. I was also relishing the parade of men and the gay fashion statements that wouldn't even be fashion whispers in my mid-Michigan town.

During one morning address, Michael Denneny, my editor at St. Martin's Press at the time, was urging writers to actively help build their own careers. A publisher can't create an audience, Denneny said; a writer has to do that, and by doing readings. It made perfect sense to me. I was electrified by the idea of not being passive when my book of short stories came out the following fall. Instead of waiting to see what my publisher would do and what might happen, I could take steps myself, take charge. I turned to Gersh and said, "We can do that, can't we?"

I suppose he could have slapped me, or said, "I'm busy this decade," or just pretended not to hear me. But he got excited too, and so our combination bake sale/crusade began. We had no idea what was in store.

At readings, being handed checks or cash by mistake has made me very uncomfortable, although I haven't had to make change. When people inviting me to come read at their schools or synagogues ask me to bring copies of my books, I'm instantly reminded of one of my parents' friends, Mr. Sorkin, a shirt salesman. I picture myself burdened with a huge, black, wheeled sample case. . . .

In the beginning, when I showed up at a bookstore, I expected an attractive or at least visible window display, with a sign of some kind and artfully arranged copies of my book. But sometimes there

was almost nothing, or what was in the window was so boring and unappealing I felt like I was looking at a window display for trusses, walkers, and orthopedic hose.

At one store, Gersh squinted at a dreary arrangement of my books atop a low bookcase and suddenly started rearranging it like a jaunty chef on a TV cooking show. In a few minutes, the display was attractive and eye-catching. He shrugged at my surprise. "Somebody had to do it," he said matter-of-factly.

Equally as disappointing as poor displays, at first, was the ring of cash registers and phones. I learned that bookstores can't afford to close down for an hour or even a half-hour while an author reads. Just as strange as the noise was having browsers idle right by while I read, either not looking, or looking and listening for a bit, and then moving on. I felt publicly branded as boring.

At one bookstore I was squeezed into a corner formed by two long shelves—making the point of a triangle. I felt claustrophobic and trapped, and worried what my body looked like in perspective. Even worse was reading in a bookstore in front of a wall of erotic greeting cards.

There have been other discomforts. My collection's title has Hebrew in it, referring to the Jewish fast day that memorializes the Roman destruction of the Temple in Jerusalem. That Hebrew can lead to trouble when I'm introduced. *Dancing on Tisha B'Av* has been called "Dancing on Tisha B'Avenue," "Dancing on Tisha Bay," "Dancing on Tisha Baja," "Dancing on Trisha B'Av," and even "Dancing on the Tissue Box."

Before reading a story, I like to talk about coming out as a gay man and as a Jewish man, and afterward I like to take questions. So I give out a lot of information about myself—which probably encourages readers to assume the stories are even more autobiographical than they might in fact be. This has led to odd interactions. Because one of my Jewish characters is uncircumcised, someone asked if *I* was. I told him to check with my editor.

Most people are less intrusive when they speak to me after a reading and ask me to sign their books, although I was thrown by the enthusiastic reader who demanded I write something funny in Yiddish in her book; I ended up barely able to write in English. Occasionally someone will gush over my work and then compare me to Writer X, whom I despise. I've learned to smile and just say thanks.

"Why should I buy this book?" some people have asked at bookstores, and I'm generally dumbfounded. The best response was offered by a witty friend after a reading from *Dancing on Tisha B'Av* at Lambda Rising in Washington, DC. He pointed out to a hesitant buyer, "Really, the hardcover's a bargain at sixteen ninety-five—that's only about ninety cents a story."

And a sale was made, but I decided then and there that my second collection would have no story under a dollar.

I've been asked to prove that my book has "something to say to women" and have been chastised for writing about people "unfamiliar" to the reader. Being gay and Jewish has also led to a confusion of identities. Dining with sponsors of my reading at a New England university, I was surprised when a latecomer gushed, "I loved *Equal Affections!* "That's by David Leavitt," I pointed out as the table fell silent. "I'm Lev Raphael." Plunging ahead, the woman said, "Oh, but both of you are gay and Jewish, right?" Someone else at the table piped up, "Well, that's true, but in Lev's fiction, you can *tell*."

But despite some bizarre and even dispiriting experiences out on the road, the tour was mostly positive, even exciting in ways I couldn't have imagined. Reading a story for an audience, I enter it in a completely different way, inhabiting it now, whereas before it inhabited me. I listen to myself with a double consciousness—examining how I respond to the story when read aloud, and how others respond. I see that some lines don't work as well as I thought, and some scenes play better than I realized. I edit as I read, and each reading teaches me how to tackle the next one.

Doing retail *could* be worse.

Scars

I

My father even criticized the way I walked and stood. Out on the street—out on Broadway. "Walk like *this*." And he'd put his feet out train-track straight, stride and march.

One-hundred-fiftieth Street and Broadway, Harlem now, Washington Heights when I grew up. How many people watched him stop me and demonstrate?

Was I pigeon-toed? I can't remember which way my feet were turned. But they weren't turned his way. I didn't walk like him. I wasn't him—was that his gripe?

Or, leaning against a counter or a wall, my feet turned in, balanced on each inner edge—I liked how it felt—he'd badger me to stand up straight. Was it bad for my flat feet? For my shoes? I never understood. That was the problem. I couldn't understand his rules, his standards, his demands.

As a little boy I was mystified by cars, by my father in a car. He demanded we stop talking when he turned the key in the ignition, as if our silence protected us—or him—like goggles from the glare of an atomic test. What did it mean? What did any of them mean, these crazy rules?

Thirty-five years later, he hasn't changed. Watches me pouring milk over cereal. Under his eye, I pour too much, of course.

Flatly he says, "Oh. You like so much milk?"

Well, not always, but see, I forgot to use my measuring cup to get the right proportion of flake to liquid. . . . My smart-ass retort goes unshared. Instead, I reply as if he's asked a sensible and interesting question, as if we're having a conversation and I'm not on trial.

Another time, a few years earlier. I'm in my thirties, at my parents' cramped and grimy Forest Hills kitchen where the glossy walls are flecked with stove-top grease. He watches me empty an ice tray on a narrow counter. "That's how you do it?" Almost always there's a question that implies I'm wrong. Almost always I want to flare up but stifle my annoyance. Sometimes I can laugh, imagine that he's kidding me.

These small domestic moments are continual episodes in my disgrace. I never meet his expectations, whatever they are. Even when I do well, he finds a way to savage my composure.

In college, acting in *Measure for Measure,* enjoying myself. His only comment is, "How come he walks so quietly on the stage? At home, he's like an elephant."

Yes, that's me, noisy, clumsy, loud, unathletic, the old me buried today under the well-built man who lifts weights, talks about trainers, food programs, protein, vascularity, and body composition. The bullied little boy is along for the ride, glad of my protection.

II

A *vildeh chaya*, he called me, a "wild animal" in Yiddish, because I was loud, defiant, sarcastic. When he spanked me, I screamed so much I made him sick, ashamed. Knowing his weakness, unconsciously (and loving to make noise), I screamed before he even touched me, ran screaming down the long hallway to hide under my bed, where he'd have to drag me out.

My mother found my racket comforting. "I always knew where you were in the house when you were little." And we smiled at this.

But my father called me "stupid" because of my noise, my silliness, my aping what he said and how he said it. I was dramatically defiant. Unlike my brother Sam, whose revolutions skulked behind a placid wall—vandalism, fighting, drugs.

His nickname for me, "Stupid," became a brand, so ineradicable that in my freshman year of college, I called Kris, the first professor to ever give me an A, to find out if she really thought I deserved it.

And not just "stupid." In English: "A mouth like a garbage can." I was disgusted but pleased—the cans I thought of were big and steel and hard to crush.

"Azah moyl"—Such a mouth—but the translation doesn't capture his dry contempt.

And even now, despite the years of public speaking, I can wonder after a party (even my own): did I talk too much?

III

Was I an angry child? My mother said I sang and smiled. She also said I threw wooden figures from the Belgian Congo out my bedroom window. I remember pissing in the metal kitchen garbage can, the echoed hit and hiss. I poured salt into *latkes* frying on the stove and spoiled their taste.

I was an angry adolescent, cursing, screaming at my brother who seemed as tyrannical as my father, but unfairly. Wasn't he also a son?

Am I angry now? Unfair?

Because my father must have laughed with me, at least when I was very young and bathed with him, and splashed.

Is all of this a settling of accounts, now that his face is eating through my own?

My mother said that boys my age who came into the store looked up to him, sought his advice.

I never did.

IV

Describing him is difficult. There is his general effect on me: intimidation, envy, shame. There is the slightly pathetic older man he has become. There is the recent immigrant of my childhood, the man staring out impassive from one 1950s black and white Kodak after another, unsmiling giant of my youth (though never tall). Bright red hair, gray eyes, freckles, with the build and hard, brooding handsomeness of Dana Andrews. (Is that why *Laura* has such a hold on me?) Is it my own fantasy that my father, mostly cold, was a warm and passionate man inside, smitten, moved?

With crude poetry, this is how he described meeting my mother in Germany after World War II, after their concentration camps were liberated: "I saw her. She was mine, I was hers." Nothing else.

Hearing this, I was too young and stunned to even ask what he meant. Their love was fated? Immediate? Or—they had sex? That day, that week? I see a picture of them on a Belgian beach, standing side by side, and he is closer to the lens. His swim suit bulges, her breasts are large and full.

Who is this man who chose a German Shepherd as his dog? A gentle dog, but he named it Rippy, Rip.

What could it mean to walk this dog, to feed and brush and bathe the type of dog the Germans used against men like him? Surely dogs like this had growled and snarled at him, threatened to rip his throat apart. And now he led one on a leash, now he was the master.

I have written about him again and again, reflections, shards. The opening of my first published story:

Marc's father had an odd, stubborn way of standing: His hands were inevitably in his pockets and all of him seemed to lean forward, as if he'd placed himself in your path and the next move were up to *you*. In his father's presence Marc often felt as if he had to excuse himself; one look of those narrow grey eyes would put him so much on the defensive that even a "hello" could come out apologetically. Ten minutes alone with his father could exhaust Marc. Luckily, his father rarely spoke to him.

Reading this now, it seems too tame. No hint of thuggery, no sneers, no shaking disappointed head. Back then, perhaps I thought there'd come a time when we could talk, be close, and so I muffled who he was.

In those 1950s snapshots he looks sullen, maybe trapped. But why?

I'm nineteen when he reveals he wanted to leave us many times. But my brother topped that revelation years later: "Dad told me he wanted to jump in the Hudson when they got to New York—he couldn't take it." Escaping us? My mother? Or just life? These bombs of truth flatten me.

V

My father has left me scarred. There's a photo of the four of us, I'm an infant, plastic nipple in my mouth, bandage across my head, lying in my mother's arms. She looks down and smiles. My father stands apart, in short-sleeved shirt and pleated pants. The story: My mother said she asked him to put me to bed, several times, because I looked tired. I fell somehow against the glass-topped blond wood coffee table, ripping open an eyebrow, needing stitches. I have the scar—a line, a space where nothing grows. I see that fifties room—the archway to the foyer, the double French doors to the dining room, the smaller one to the hall. The olive rug, the thick and heavy chairs and couch, in green or red shot through with gold; the bulky matching drapes and ugly driftwood lamps. I see it all but have no memories. I have the scar.

Judaism's Moral Strength

As a writer and avid magazine and newspaper reader, I've always liked to follow opinions and controversies in the letters columns of journals I read. I enjoy well-argued letters and the unexpected tidbits of information I sometimes learn from knowledgeable letter writers. But reading letters to the editor in the *Lansing State Journal,* our local paper, is often a depressing and maddening experience for me. The voices of narrow-mindedness, ignorance, and unadulterated hatred crop up far too frequently, making me feel isolated.

I'm thinking of a recent letter in the *Lansing State Journal* in which someone confidently maintained that the persecution of Jews and homosexuals in—as she confusedly put it—"postwar" Germany could not be compared. Why? Because Jews were persecuted for being Jewish, while homosexuals were persecuted for "illegal and immoral behavior."

That letter writer seemed to imply that the persecution of homosexuals—which included harassment, incarceration in concentration camps, torture, and death—is acceptable. Or at least more acceptable than persecuting Jews.

To make such a statement is to blame the victim, and we Jews should be sensitive to such rhetorical tricks, since we have been falsely accused by some writers of having participated in our own slaughter during World War II, and even of having encouraged it in some obscene way.

Thousands of homosexuals were persecuted and murdered by the Nazis because the Nazis were sick and full of hate. It is the behavior and identity of the *murderers* that counts, not the victims, because the Nazis targeted different groups for discrimination, imprisonment, or death at different times: Jehovah's Witnesses, labor union leaders, epileptics, women, Catholics, Gypsies, Communists, the mentally retarded, Poles. Anyone could have been crushed by the Nazi Moloch for reasons of policy. Though Jews were always the Nazis' prime target, anyone could be made vulnerable and ruled outside of the law.

Yes, homosexual activity was illegal in Germany *before* Hitler. But the Nazis further restricted and punished it in their complete perversion of German law and life in which scapegoating and hounding Jews was paramount. In 1933 laws were passed to ban Jews from the legal professions and civil service; groups promoting homosexual rights were banned that same year. The 1935 Nuremberg laws eliminated Jews' civil rights and citizenship and banned intermarriage and sexual contacts between Jews and non-Jews. That very year widened restrictions on homosexuals, such as banning gay bars, made it more possible to legally target homosexuals for persecution. Conditions for German Jews grew steadily harsher and ended in catastrophe, but perhaps less well known—especially to Jews—is the parallel persecution of homosexuals. That sad history is well documented in books like Richard Plant's *The Pink Triangle*, praised by no less a writer than Holocaust historian

Martin Gilbert. It would be a mistake for me to sneeringly shrug off evidence of prejudice like that letter in the *Lansing State Journal* and say, "Well, that's Lansing, what can you expect from a town that thinks it's a city?" What can you expect from what my parents would pungently call in Yiddish a *lochovich* (a nowhere town)?

A real mistake. Because the bigoted voices I encounter in the *Lansing State Journal* are sometimes echoed in our supposedly more sophisticated and tolerant Jewish community. With no sense of history, letters in the *Detroit Jewish News* have called for death to homosexuals, as the Torah seems to urge.

The link of Jews and homosexuals is one that makes some Jews extremely uncomfortable. Understandably so, up to a point. When many Jews hear any other group mentioned as having been targeted in the Holocaust, they rightly fear that the specific nature of Jewish suffering and destruction will be blurred. That the Shoah will simply be classed as another example of human brutality, and Jews will suffer a second historical erasure.

But this fear can lead to bizarre and irrational behavior. To speak of Jews and homosexuals as victims of the Nazis does no dishonor to Jews, does not in any way decrease the significance of the catastrophe for Jews. Yet too many Jews recoil in disgust and horror, or get enraged when the subject comes up.

Jewish communities have historically encouraged and admired learning and wisdom, so it is particularly disturbing when Jews, of all people, parade ignorance and intolerance as knowledge. I had ample opportunity to observe aspects of this behavior when I toured the country in 1991 and 1992 promoting *Dancing on Tisha B'Av*.

In one city, I learned that organizers of a Holocaust memorial commemoration absolutely refused to allow a non-Jewish gay man to light one of the six memorial candles. The reasons were many but overlapping: it was not his place to be there, it was not appropriate, how could you say what happened to Jews and gays was the same? But the rage underneath these assertions was telling. How dare he put himself forward, how dare any homosexual claim the right to participate in this ceremony! I have attended Holocaust memorial ceremonies where a number of groups are listed along with Jews, but never homosexuals.

In another city, I ran into a wall when I spoke at a Jewish community center with Evelyn Torton Beck, editor of the groundbreaking *Nice Jewish Girls: A Lesbian Anthology*. She is the child of survivors, as I am, and she is a lesbian. I was dumbfounded when we met informally with a group of children of survivors who asked point-blank why we "had to be gay" that evening. Why couldn't we set it aside?

When you're in a Christian group, we asked, do you set your Jewishness aside, isn't that always a part of your identity?

They didn't see the connection. Our multiple identities as Jews, children of survivors, and homosexuals seemed to embarrass and even confuse them. And they wouldn't admit that the rabid hatred directed at lesbians and gays by some in the Jewish community *is* hatred.

"It's religion," they insisted, sounding as petulant to me as students defending an indefensible statement with the sullen claim, "It's my opinion, it doesn't have to be right."

Lies are lies. Hatred is hatred. As Jews, we know what it sounds and feels and smells and tastes like. Those of us who haven't experienced it directly know others who have.

And when a New York rabbi went to Oregon to support and defend the right-wing activists who wanted to enlist state government in limiting the rights of gays and lesbians and actively discouraging homosexuality—and he claimed religious authority—that, too, was hatred, plain and simple. This same rabbi claimed that comparing Oregon's Measure 9 to Nazi laws against the Jews was the act of "ignorant people." Clearly, his zealotry made him ignorant of what is indisputable historical fact: the Nazis' legal and murderous campaign of persecution against Jews *and* homosexuals.

Likewise, controversy recently erupted in Detroit's Jewish community about the whole question of rabbis performing commitment ceremonies for gay and lesbian Jews. Ridiculous and bigoted claims were made about gay and lesbian Jews and about homosexuality—by *rabbis,* our supposed leaders.

One rabbi said that homosexuals "define themselves by their sexuality." Another said that same-sex Jewish commitment ceremonies would promote "a lifestyle of instinctual gratification which is not channeled or sublimated toward a greater objective." In other, cruder words: all that gay people think about or want is sex; they have no life outside of sex.

This charge is exactly the same kind of vicious calumny that anti-Semites have historically directed at Jews: they say we're only interested in money. Both claims are absurd, disgusting, and dangerous, because they lead from stereotyping to violence of attitude and action. Furthermore, calling gayness a "lifestyle" trivializes something very complex (sexual identity), reducing it to faddishness.

These responses remind me of a poignant passage in Joseph Beam's black gay anthology *In the Life:*

> I cannot go home as who I am. When I speak of home, I
> mean not only the familial constellation from which I grew,
> but the entire Black community, the Black press, the Black
> church, Black academicians, the Black literati, and the Black
> left. Where is my reflection? I am most often rendered invis-
> ible, perceived as a threat to the family, or am tolerated if I
> am silent and inconspicuous. I cannot go home as who I am
> and that hurts me deeply.

What, then, is the answer? Rabbi Michael Sternfield of Congregation Beth Israel in San Diego has dealt beautifully and clearly with outrageous and destructive Jewish claims about homosexuality. In an Erev Rosh Hashanah sermon, he urged his congregation:

> We need a Judaism which *includes;* a Judaism which is expan-
> sive and outreaching; a Judaism which recognizes the
> inherent dignity and worth in life of each person. This means
> that as a community, we must do our very best to include not
> only gays and lesbians, but also *single* Jews, *poor* Jews, *divorced*

Jews, Jews with *physical* and *mental* disabilities, Jews who are *intermarried*—in other words, all of those of our people who seem not to conform to the theoretical model. . . . Jews, better than most, should understand the bitterness of *ostracism, suspicion* and *phobias* for we have been strangers in many lands. . . . Our attitude towards gays and lesbians is a *true test* of the depth of our commitment to the Torah's human values. Judaism's moral strength is tested not by how narrowly we may define its parameters, but rather how broadly we can draw its circle.

Almost Famous?

In John Updike's hilarious *Bech at Bay*, the author's satirical alter ego, Jewish novelist Henry Bech, goes on a murder spree in his mid-seventies. What's fueling his criminal outbreak isn't senility, but decades of rage at the reviewers who trashed his work and, as he sees it, committed "virtual murder." Like Bech, most authors can remember stinging phrases from bad reviews with as much accuracy as raves, if not more so. I know I can. But the review that's had the most devastating impact on me was one that I didn't get.

Soon after my first book of short stories, *Dancing on Tisha B'Av*, was published in 1990, I heard the unbelievably wonderful news that it was going to be reviewed in the *New York Times Book Review*. I wasn't thrilled just as an author, but also as a native New Yorker who had grown up believing that the *Times* was simply the best newspaper in the universe. Good or bad, a *Times* review was the ultimate imprimatur; until the *Times* recognized you, you didn't exist as a writer.

The report of this impending joy came on the rainy fall evening that I was in New York to launch a reading tour for my book. A novelist friend who had blurbed my collection—and was introducing me at a Greenwich Village bookstore reading that evening—greeted me with an exciting announcement: he'd just gotten a call from the *Times* asking him to review the book. I could hardly breathe out my reply: "And?"

He shrugged. "I said I knew you too well and it was a conflict of interest. They're asking someone else. The review should be out fairly soon." We both grinned a bit sheepishly.

It was only afterward, long afterward, that I wished I'd shouted, "Call them back! Say it was another Lev Raphael you were thinking of! Say you'll do the review!"

Fueled by the enthusiastic crowd at the bookstore, and by the news, my reading was a success, and its glow stayed with me on the ensuing book tour and every week from that evening on as I opened up the *Book Review*, waiting to see my name and the title of my book. I now know that if I were going to be reviewed, my agent and my publisher would have found out a week in advance, but to me, a beginner, the *New York Times* was as magnificently mysterious as the black obelisk in *2001: A Space Odyssey*.

Weeks passed, then months. The reviews rolled in from across the country, even from the London *Times*, but nothing in New York. I pestered my editor. He had no idea what had gone wrong and told me there was absolutely no way of finding out: "They're as secretive as the Vatican over there," he explained. My writer friends came up with various scenarios: the review had been killed because it was too negative, or because it was too positive; maybe it was badly written; maybe it was never reassigned or written at all and simply fell through the cracks after the first phone call. Most of my friends had not been reviewed in the *Times* either, but none had seen the hot promise of a review there turn cold.

Still, I didn't despair completely, because I kept seeing reviews of other books appear long after the books they discussed had been published. Surely there was hope for me?

But after nine months of fruitless waiting, I gave up. I felt as confounded as the builders of the Tower of Babel who had aimed too high. How could I have expected to be reviewed in the *Times*? Who did I think I was? It was supremely humiliating, too, after having told so many friends and colleagues that I was going to be reviewed in the *Times*. Why couldn't I have kept my mouth shut?

I got so depressed I eventually had to stop reading the *Book Review*. When the Sunday paper came, I would slip that section out, tear it in half, and throw it in the garbage. Even that precaution didn't always work, because it seemed to emit noxious fumes of shame, and I'd have to put it out with the trash in the garage so as to have more walls between us.

On the few occasions I made the mistake of even glancing inside the *Book Review*, perhaps vainly willing myself to be over the disappointment, I'd either find reviews of books by people I knew or advertisements for their work—and sometimes both. Every printed line seemed a face in a jeering crowd that mocked my failure. An essayist friend here in Michigan has coined a phrase for the long, gray Michigan winters in which other people's lives seem brighter and more successful: he calls them "The Envy Months." For me, that season of overcast emotional skies became perpetual.

I went on to publish a novel, a book of essays and memoirs, a study of Edith Wharton's life and fiction, four coauthored books in psychology and education, and an academic mystery, but still the unanswerable question haunted me: why wasn't my first book reviewed? And more haunting still: what would have happened if the review had appeared? How would it have changed my stock in the publishing world?

Then, in the fall of 1997 the unbelievable finally happened, and it was not a disappointment. One Monday afternoon I heard the thin ring of the fax and approached warily. I'd had my share of bad news come over the fax line, and often when it rang I recalled Dorothy Parker's pungent question, "What fresh hell is this?" But what unreeled from the fax machine this day was paradisal: a copy of Marilyn Stasio's "Crime" column from the coming week's *New York Times Book Review*, with a paragraph bracketed and a jubilant note from my agent.

I read it quietly. I read it several times. I tried to absorb the fact that here at last was a review of one of my books—and placed right after the review of Martha Grimes's new mystery! And it was not just any review. Stasio, the country's most important mystery reviewer, had given my second academic mystery, *The Edith Wharton Murders*, a flat-out rave that would make for great pull-quotes. I was finally on the map, and my exultation erupted in shouting, jumping up and down, a flurry of phone calls, a purchase of champagne, celebrating, and then more celebrating. After seven years, I was determined to keep enjoying this triumph as long as possible. When the review actually appeared in the paper, I had it blown up and framed so that I could see it every time I went into my study to work.

And the results of this success were immediate. Library sales of the book doubled, it went into a second printing, and the publisher was bombarded with requests for review copies. Mystery writer friends told me they'd never been reviewed by Marilyn Stasio, even after a dozen books. As the glow faded, I realized how very fortunate I was to have been singled out this time. Because once was enough; even if I never got reviewed in the *Times* again, the review could be quoted for the rest of my writing career. As my partner wryly said, "They won't take it back."

Indeed they didn't, and an excerpted version ran when the paperback came out, and friends around the country reported they saw the book facing out in both literature as well as mystery sections.

Did that review and its postscript eclipse the one I never got? I wish I could say yes, that the pain of my first major disappointment has been completely healed. I don't know if anything ever makes up for a lost opportunity early in your career.

But my career took an ironic turn in the mid-1990s, when I became a book reviewer for the *Detroit Free Press*—with my own monthly mystery column—and a book critic for National Public Radio's *The Todd Mundt Show*. While neither venue has the clout of the *Times*, I found myself eagerly sought out as a reviewer. An editor at a major publishing house recently lamented to me that he used to expect at least a dozen reviews for a debut novel, but no longer, because review space is shrinking. And with megawriters like Patricia Cornwell guaranteed wide media coverage, new writers have less access than ever before; thus, every review they get is crucial.

The latest, unexpected turn in my career is getting my own radio show on a mid-Michigan public station: half an hour every week to interview authors and talk to listeners about new books.

So it's impossible for me not to wonder now and then, especially when I'm surveying a load of advance reading copies, if there are newly-published writers out there who are hoping and praying for me to review their work. Or even worse, feeling miserable because they thought I would, but I never got around to it.

Into His Eyes

I'm reading in my study, where books climb up every wall, and Kobi pads in, glances at me as if waiting for a nod. So I say, "Go ahead," and he jumps onto the comfortable gold velour armchair opposite me. Sometimes it seems less that he's asking for permission and more that he's simply interacting with me the way we would say Hi or touch someone's shoulder Hello.

Identical to the chair I'm in, it's his favorite chair—in this room, anyway. He has two other favorite chairs. One is a cocoa-colored Scandinavian leather recliner in the living room. The other's a small blue tub chair in the bedroom I share with my partner of twenty-one years in a heavily-treed mid-Michigan suburb filled with 1950s ranch houses.

If someone's sitting in this particular chair, he'll wait and stare, or glance at it and walk past, sit under my desk, and wait. He can be deferential at such moments, but he's very clear about what he wants. He's a Westie, and as they say, Westies will not be ignored.

He spends so much time on this chair—when he's not out terrorizing squirrels in the large back yard—that we call it "his chair." He likes to snooze up there with his head off to one side, cushioned by the end of the chair arm.

When Gersh and I leave him alone at home, we say, "Kobi, it's time to guard the house," and he heads right to that chair. When we need to de-mat him or do any other grooming and health maintenance, like brushing his teeth, we say, "Kobi, it's time for grooming," and he heads for the chair.

He could manage to jump onto it when he was tiny, but he was scared to jump off and would pace back and forth and whine. Like a father encouraging his child to dive into a pool, I would pat the thick brown rug and say, "Jump!" and praise him when he did. I'm always remembering what he used to do and used to be, because, like any parent, when I look at Kobi, the past is a pentimento, creeping out from what's on the surface. I see him at different ages whenever I look at him, so that each moment is many moments, and I enjoy who he was just as much as who he is right now.

He also takes me to other times. When Gersh and I attended a conference for gay and lesbian Jews in Israel in the early nineties, we were struck by one attendee's name: Kobi. A nickname for Yakov (Jacob). Then and there we decided we'd name our dog Kobi whenever we got one. Kobi came into our life not long after my mother died, and I was still in mourning and deeply depressed about my career, which was in a periodic slump. Having him to focus on brought me out of myself in a healing, constructive way. And one day early in our life together, when I bent down to kiss the top of Kobi's head, I remembered my mother doing the same thing to me when I was a little boy and half-ironically murmuring the Yiddish for "A blessing on your head." Did she send him to me? I like to think so.

Sometimes Kobi sits up in his chair after he's climbed onto it, looking at me, and it's clear he wants something. To be petted or spoken to. I'll stop what I'm doing to comply. Then he lets go, lies down, and disappears into sleep. If he's a bit restless, I give him a hand signal from my chair, my right hand out, palm down, lowering it as I say, "Rest, rest." It's what we did when we were crate-training him as a puppy and he needed to get used to being in his crate at night. Only back then, we lay down outside his crate to mimic what we wanted him to do. We were doting, dotty parents.

But it paid off, because now it always works. As if he's being hypnotized, his eyes start to flutter shut with each "Rest," and he sinks down into the chair. His chair.

Today, however, he doesn't need the coaxing, he needs something else. Though he seems to be settling in for a snooze, his eyes are still wide open. I meet his gaze, hold it, and we stare into each other's eyes as we have been doing ever since he was a six-pound puppy. It goes on for half a minute. It goes on forever.

"I love you," I say quietly, as I did when he first came into our lives, over and over, and slowly his eyelids droop and he falls asleep. In their dog training books, the Monks of New Skete strongly believe that accustoming your puppy to more and more eye contact from the very beginning will lay a strong foundation for future training, but even more importantly, it will build a deeper relationship, a "real exchange between animal and man." These are moments as rich with connection as when a parent gazes into the eyes of a suckling infant and a whole world of mutuality opens up between them.

Did Kobi seek this extra level of connection right then when he looked at me from his chair, or did he just accept it? I can't be sure. But as always, I marvel at the way he is entwined around my heart.

I grew up with a pedigreed medium-sized German shepherd that we rescued from a pound at seven months, but he wasn't really my dog—he belonged to my father, adored my father. As the youngest in the family, I was tolerated and played with. I did my share of walking and feeding Rippy, and I played with him and brushed him sometimes, but I wasn't deeply involved in his upbringing or care.

Kobi is the first dog I've raised from a puppy, and I was completely unprepared for the depth of the relationship that we established with each other from the very first weeks, the sense of connection, the intimacy.

It started with his physical closeness. When we first adopted him, because he weighed about six pounds he was small enough to be held in my hands. He was also small enough to sit on me, even stretch out on me. He quickly made up his mind that sleeping on my chest when I was sprawled on the living room couch was a good thing. He'd clamber up, pad over, plop down on my chest, and tuck his chin in as close to mine as possible. As he'd fall asleep, we'd be breathing each other's breath. The scent of his coat enveloped me—a cross between popcorn and cardboard—and I felt a level of peace and contentment I'd never experienced before, as relaxed as if I were meditating. I'd wonder if being surrounded and sheltered by me was for Kobi a return to the litter, analogous to what it felt like to lie against his mother. He could even fall asleep on me if we were playing and I stretched out on the floor on my back. He would climb up, plant his chin between my pecs, and then his eyelids would start fluttering closed.

On the couch, he simply did what he wanted, and because I wanted it, too, that was fine. But just as I learned during potty training him the signs that meant he had to be whisked outside, I also soon learned to pay close attention to everything he did and "said." Our Westie breeder, Janet, would often respond to our questions about dog training by advising us to "Ask Kobi," and so we learned how to ask him, and he in turn learned how to tell us.

Like all puppies, he was curious and playful, and within the first month, he initiated a game. One evening while I was chasing him around the house, he dashed into my study and slid under a skirted hassock that hid him completely. I stood there laughing and then said, "Where's Kobi?" He poked his nose out just enough for it to be seen. I laughed even more, and it seemed he was waiting for me to do something. So I reached in and started to wrestle with him, and he play-growled and mouthed my fingers. In a few days the game developed variations. If I didn't ask, "Where's Kobi?" quickly enough, he would grunt louder and louder to get my attention. And soon I was reaching in from all sides as he twisted and turned to "get" me.

This game was something we cocreated and each can initiate. He's almost six years old now and weighs twenty-one pounds, but if I say, "Where's Kobi?" or, "Do you want to go under?" he'll slither under the hassock (it's not as comfortable a fit as it used to be). If I'm at my computer and resisting his blandishments of barking or squeaking a stuffed toy, he'll dive under the hassock, because he knows I'm guaranteed to respond. He also created the bedroom version of "Where's Kobi?" by crawling under the covers and scooting around there while play-snarling at us as we tickle him.

I didn't expect that we would be interacting like this, but the communication kept deepening, because I kept watching him, studying him, and he learned that he had a responsive audience. The first time he sat down next to his water bowl rather than drinking from it, I knew without looking that he wanted fresh water. Kobi quickly learned the words "fresh water" and started following me to the kitchen sink when I'd ask if that's what he wanted, and I refilled his dish.

He barked when he wanted to go out into the back yard, but the first time that he didn't rush out of the open door and instead reared back with one front leg up, I was sure he wanted me to come with him (the gesture even looked like an excited "After you!"). I was right, because outside he grabbed one of his yard toys and started to play "Keep away," where he grabs a toy, brandishes it at us, and runs off, daring us to get it from him. Now if I hesitate at the door when he wants a companion, he'll either push at me or refuse to go out unless I lead the way.

Our bed is too high for him to jump onto, so we keep a hassock from one of the bedroom chairs alongside it as a "ladder." Once I'd forgotten to move it over and found him sitting in the bedroom by the bed. He looked at the hassock, then looked at the bed, then looked at me. I knew what to do.

Because I work at home, I look forward to walking him through our subdivision, rich with hundred-year-old trees, but sometimes I get distracted and forget I'm out there for his health and mine, and

I walk too fast and don't allow Kobi enough sniff time. After all, smelling is the main way he experiences the world. Kobi doesn't just stop when he wants to keep sniffing, he puts a paw down on his leash, and if I still really don't get it, he puts two down and glares at me, his head lifted in what looks to me like challenge or annoyance. I listen.

Despite all the dog books I read, the Web sites I visited, and all the conversations I had with our breeder and other dog owners, something simple but beautiful was never entirely clear to me. Bringing Kobi into our home was creating a new relationship, one that evolved between us. He has taught me what he wanted, and I have taught him that when he expressed his needs, he would be understood. This has built confidence and trust between us and has made Kobi a well-adjusted, balanced dog. And one who seeks out eyes. Another Westie parent down the street is often remarking on the way Kobi is studying us, watching us.

And merging with us. As when he climbs onto our bed at night, settles down next to me, then lifts his head up and looks right into my eyes for one last shot of connection before he tucks his head in and disappears into his dream world, while I go off to mine.

Heart of Darkness?

I am flying to a country that disappointed our president about Iraq despite being a longtime ally, and I'm wondering how to hide that I'm an American, given the anti-U.S. sentiment I keep reading about.

It's May 2002. Friends have delayed or even canceled trips to Europe. They don't want to be berated by strangers about the Iraq war, or American imperialism, or the president, whether they voted for him or not. I didn't, but will people believe me?

There have been times in my life I hid being gay, and now I'm contemplating a different camouflage. I won't wear sneakers or sweats or a fanny pack—but do I go further? Sport the Canadian flag pin I was recently given at a conference in Toronto? Or something more subtle? I could wear only black—not typical American tourist garb—and try to pass myself off as somehow being European. I don't look American—people always tell me that in Europe, while they toss around nationalities. Dutch. Norwegian. Possibly German.

But it's Germany I'm headed for, and Germans will surely know I'm not one of them. Haven't they always, with my people? Won't they see it in my eyes, instantly? And this is deeper—the real fear: can I bear being a Jew, the son of Holocaust survivors, in Germany, even for less than a week?

Germany, the country I swore never to visit. The country whose products I never bought, the country that was so alien and radioactive I used to imagine maps of Europe without it. As if I were a superhero whose laser gaze could slice it away from the continent and sink it without a trace. Then Switzerland would have a seacoast. Austria, too.

And I would have revenge for the camps and killing squads that not only murdered dozens of my parents' relatives, but poisoned their memories as well. Talking about their lost parents, cousins, aunts, uncles was so painful for my own parents that I have no family tree to climb to in middle age, no names and professions and cities to study and explore. The Nazis certainly won that round—like a giant grinding his victim's bones to dust.

Growing up in New York, I bristled on buses and in the subway if I heard someone old enough to have been a camp guard or Nazi soldier speaking German. *Were you there?* I wondered. And now I am studying a phrase book, *Just Enough German,* trying to speak the tongue that ordered my family to death.

Asking where the toilet or train station is seems easy enough, just enough, and then I come to food terms. A rare steak is *blutig.* Bloody. I toss the book down, remembering my mother quoting the first line of a Nazi anthem: *Wenn Judenblutt vom Messer spritzt.* They were never just words to me, none of it was just words or books. Jewish blood did splash from German knives.

I used to joke, darkly, that my nightmare was a plane crashing in Germany—and my surviving, having to stay in a German hospital, surrounded by Them.

Yet this is the country I am flying to by choice. I am researching a memoir about my mother, and very distant cousins of hers live in Magdeburg, in the east.

It is beyond irony, since this is the city where my mother was a slave laborer for almost a year in Polte Fabrik, Germany's largest munitions factory, which used slave laborers from the Buchenwald concentration camp. In addition to hunger and daily factory accidents, she and her fellow prisoners suffered frequent bombardments that cut off food supplies and diminished their already meager meals. Death threatened them in more bizarre ways: a doctor took X rays, which she misread and thus consigned people she thought were tubercular to quicker extermination.

Magdeburg is on the Elbe, a river filled with Jewish bodies, my mother said, killed in a hurry by the Germans as the Soviets and Americans descended from east and west.

This is my intimate geography.

In Germany, however, I'm studying a Eurorail map. And without even knowing it, I have slipped into tourism. Intrigued, I note everything different, whether the tile roofs or the tiny cars. I enjoy the comfortable trains with good service. And I try my hand at speaking the bits of German I have had time to practice, while picking up more words and phrases with surprising speed.

Magdeburg, clean and open and dull, is a city of loss. The population has declined by tens of thousands since before the war and then again since reunification. Dozens of ruined churches were torn down by the Russians. Grand baroque streets have disappeared into wide barren boulevards.

Yet there are more parks here than in any other German city, I am told, and my hosts live in a sunny new house with a large open-style American kitchen. Everything I eat there, and elsewhere, is delicious.

Before I visit the site of Polte Fabrik, I discuss the camp and factory with my hosts and an intense graduate student in history at the local university, who is doing his master's thesis on the Polte. One phrase of his keeps ringing in my ears. He refers to Polte as "an episode in the history of National Socialism."

And for the first time, I see my mother—even myself—as part of history.

As for the Iraq war, it hardly comes up. We are immersed in an older war that seems more real.

All that is left of the camp whose conditions the local Jewish community leader says were "terrible," even compared to others, is a damaged wooden gate flanked by brick. Polte Fabrik itself, across the street, is a series of hulking brick buildings now occupied by Magdeburg's municipal courts.

I leave Magdeburg with a pile of photocopied documents to be translated and photos waiting to be uploaded. Maybe it's naive or hopelessly American (my mother thought the two synonymous), but I want to return to Magdeburg, to see new friends again. And to visit more of Germany without this time talking or thinking about my mother's war, to enjoy the people, the sights, to listen.

I've been so busy that it's only on the quiet train taking me west that it comes to me: I not only grew up speaking Yiddish, which is strongly linked to German, but I also lived in a heavily German-Jewish neighborhood. And so the sound of German around me here, in Germany, is not remotely threatening. I enjoy it. I feel at home.

A Writer High and Low

When you have writer friends, they're often coming out with gloomy pronouncements. After one publisher cut its list, a friend at this major house who had not been cut called me and said without preamble, "Omigod, Lev! There are bodies floating down the river." Luckily I had already heard the news from someone else, so I knew what she meant and didn't assume she was hallucinating.

Another novelist friend struggling with his large publisher about all kinds of issues complained to me, "You know, the only thing worse than not being published is *being* published." And I understood: after years of trying to get a book into the world, having it published exposed him to a whole new set of disappointments and frustrations. We all know what they can be.

I've been publishing fiction and essays for over twenty-five years and books for fifteen years, sixteen of them in all. In that time, my own views of publishing and publishers have changed a great deal. Let me tell you how.

While Michigan has been home for almost half my life, I was born in New York City and I grew up with New York-sized fantasies of success. Whether you like it or not, you breathe that in along with the exhaust from lumbering buses, and it's just as toxic.

So you assume, if you want to be a writer, that you'll be published by one of the big publishers. That's a given. Your advance will be big, too. You'll be reviewed in the *New York Times,* twice—the book review and the daily paper—in *The New Yorker, New York* magazine, profiled, interviewed, photographed, on local TV news at the very least, and every radio station except for, say, Latvian reggae. The ads will be everywhere you look, the book will be piled high in every book store window, and people will talk about you as much as the weather, the Mets, or the mayor. But first and foremost, there's the famous publisher with imperial clout.

Not a very healthy set of expectations at all. And not very realistic, either, in my specific case, since my idol was Henry James and I was writing short stories from high school on. Short fiction seldom rockets anyone to the top.

At twenty-four, in the MFA program at the University of Massachusetts, then ranked one of the country's best, I won the Harvey Swados prize. The judge was famed editor Martha Foley of *Story* magazine and *The Best American Short Stories,* and her kudos were deeply encouraging. The whole thing was a bit of a vindictive triumph since my fellow workshop students and the leader hated the story, especially the end, and when I told this to Martha Foley, she growled: "Don't change a goddamned word."

So I had my literary triumph, but unfortunately, a year later, the story was published in *Redbook*—with an illustration, even. I made a lot of money, got fan mail and queries from other magazines. The unfortunate side of all this was that it seemed so easy. I'd written the story in a weekend; surely I could do one a month and really get established? My head wasn't just turned, it was spinning like Linda Blair's in *The Exorcist.*

Six years followed in which I was unable to sell a single story. I lived through six years of manila envelopes, sometimes two or three at a time, falling out of my apartment building mailbox. Of course, it was my own fault, since I thought that the only magazines worth publishing in were national ones that paid big bucks, and those were the only ones I submitted to.

But leaving New York and moving to Michigan in 1981 changed my focus, turned me inward, and for the first time in my life I asked who was my audience, not where could I make a lot of money and get exposure. It sounds simple, but it was a profound change and it helped me get published again and stay published. My main subject at the time was children of Holocaust survivors, and not surprisingly, regional Jewish magazines and journals were eager for what I wrote.

I published more and more short stories every year until 1990, after which I did a few books with St. Martin's Press. Given the reality of that press, my expectations were kept within reason and life seemed good. Okay, I wasn't famous, I wasn't making much money, I wasn't a New York–size star, I hadn't even been reviewed in the *New York Times* (though the *London* and *LA Times* did review me), but I was published and reviewed. I settled down with that reality.

Then in 1995, I and my partner sold a co-authored book to Doubleday and I went a little nuts. Neither of us had made much money or gotten very well known from publishing, so it felt to both of us that we'd hit the big time. Selling a book to Doubleday was surely the answer to our dreams: recognition in the publishing world and financial stability.

We were profoundly disappointed. The non-negotiable advance was less than half what we hoped for. With two kids in college, all it did was help us get a little further out of debt. But our agent assured us that Doubleday, with its fabulous distribution, would really stand behind the book, and a cheerful meeting with the head of publicity fed that delusion. She wanted to know if we were *Oprah* material and seemed to think we were. We even got a "side letter" to our contract which mentioned a book tour, radio and TV talk shows, and advertising in national magazines.

Our editor was so enthusiastic about the revisions we did on the manuscript that he even suggested a sequel. And a calendar. And a date book.

Then things turned sour. They produced a terrible cover (Doubleday is known for this) and wouldn't take our input at all when we had comments. And when we suggested a big name to do a blurb, someone they hadn't thought of or ever approached before, they were thrilled and complimented us for a great choice. Then they had this public figure blurb one of their other books with a much higher profile than ours.

The sucker punch was next. We were hit with devastating news a few months before the book was due out: the five-city tour was being canceled with no explanation. No one called us. We heard the news by fax.

We were powerless. Our agent told us that the side letter was basically worthless. The most tangible thing Doubleday would do by way of publicity was send out postcards, though they tried convincing us they were still supporting the book. They never did even that—we never saw any postcards.

As a reviewer, I know immediately from a press kit whether the publisher is pushing the book heavily or not, and anyone getting our press release and the galley would have known Doubleday wasn't expecting the book to do well. And it didn't.

Why were we originally set up to think that Doubleday strongly believed in our book, and then effectively dumped? I don't know, but since that time I've learned from authors, agents, even editors that shafting authors was standard operating procedure for a big house like Doubleday, and other big houses. Our editor did leave soon after our book was published, so we may have fallen victim to changes higher up.

That same year, I published a book with Faber (which had not yet been sold). Faber promised me very little, and my editor made it clear that they didn't advertise. However, I'd studied Faber and knew that what I could count on was an attractive, well-produced book, and that pleased me. I'd sold Faber the book in three weeks, negotiated the contract on my own, and was satisfied that this collection of essays would be out and available to readers of my fiction.

I was invited to a sales conference to present my book. Then came the big surprise. Faber ended up sending me to do readings in New York and Washington, DC. The irony of these disparate experiences is that when Doubleday made its offer, I didn't have a choice—it was the only one on the table, and they knew it. But with Faber, I was the one making the choice.

It's easy for writers to let their fantasies of success lead them astray, but my expectations were reasonable in both cases. It was Doubleday's double-dealing that set me up for one of the greatest disappointments I've had in my writing career, and taught me the dangers of working with a conglomerate. Of course, that's even more of a problem almost ten years later when there's been further consolidation in publishing.

In the late 1990s, when I was offered the chance to move my mystery series from St. Martin's Press, now owned by von Holtzbrinck, to the independent Walker, and for more money, I took it. Like Faber, Walker was terrific to work with and I had more input on my first cover than ever before. I actually got to speak to the art director. When I told this to a friend at a larger house, she hissed like a deflating tire and said she had never spoken to anyone in any art department—after ten books. Walker also sent me on a six-city tour and strategized in depth with me, respecting my years of experience on the road and in bookstores.

I published my most recent novel, *The German Money*, with Leapfrog Press, the smallest publisher I've ever worked with, and the most enjoyable. I was convinced that only an independent press could do justice to my new book, and I chose Leapfrog because I'd seen a few of their books, liked the production, and what's more important, their taste. It's been an amazing experience, and the level of professionalism is the highest of any publisher I've worked with.

The bedrock of our relationship has been editing. My editor, who isn't overwhelmed by the number of books he's putting out, has had time to do smart line editing and structural editing that made me take my book to a deeper level. It's also made me fall in love with my book all over again.

My editor responds to e-mails often within hours, and throughout our correspondence, I've felt deeply involved in every step of the process, my opinion as a reviewer and author not just taken seriously, but solicited.

The German Money is about children of a Holocaust survivor shocked by the contents of her will. Since I've read widely in the past at Jewish book fairs and universities, I raised with Leapfrog the idea of an early press release, targeted to this same audience. Ira Wood thought this was a good idea. He produced the best-written and most effective press release I've ever had. That release and cover letter helped me get the book adopted by the Jewish Book Council, whose president told me she'd already had more requests for me to speak in the fall than I could possibly handle.

If I thought Walker was remarkable about covers, Leapfrog outdid them. Our connection was so smooth and productive (as if we were jazzmen riffing), the publisher sent me six different early designs and asked me to rank them. I felt honored to be brought in so early, and pleased that we both liked the same design. He's been indefatigable in pushing this book out into the world and sold British/Commonwealth rights faster than any other publisher has done for me. And he decided to do postcards, which really did get produced and are beautiful. A German publisher bought the book, and two others, and has sent me on a two-week tour of Germany and Austria. Not so surprisingly, the publisher, Parthas Verlag, was founded in Berlin eight years ago as a way of introducing a cultural counterweight to the increasingly mono-lithic German publishing scene.

After all these years in publishing, I feel like I'm finally getting a big break, but it's not the flashy kind that makes it into *People* magazine. It's more solid than that: my fiction is truly being valued, beautifully edited and produced, and marketed by someone with real business savvy.

Twenty-seven years as a published writer have taught me that being an author is a hazardous enterprise, an arena of life where it would be best to inject your self-esteem with novocaine if such a thing were possible. A career is as unpredictable as the stock market: exhilarating on some days, crushing on others. Anne Perry said in the preface to a book on writing by Donald Maass "that if you write a book people want to read, it will sell," and many writing guides offer similarly cheerful pronouncements.

In today's climate, however, having something to say doesn't mean that people will necessarily listen, or, more accurately, that you'll be able to get past the gatekeepers, the editors, editorial boards, or publishers unwilling to tackle something new or risky. Forget new and risky; everyone's looking for a blockbuster, a high-concept book, say, like *The Silence of the Lambs* meets *The Adventures of Huckleberry Finn:* a thriller about a raft of serial killings.

But independent presses are willing to take risks for a simple reason: books still matter to them. Deeply.

A few years ago, Frank Rich wrote about *The Matrix* and said we're all caught in a real cultural communications matrix ourselves, created by the half-dozen corporations like Time/Warner that control what news we see and hear, what we read, what we know. Publishing has become something like that, so next time you watch *Matrix Reloaded*, think of Morpheus as an independent publisher and Neo as his latest author. It'll give it a nice spin. The black leather is optional.

Now, remember that author friend who complained about the misery of being published?

After everything I've seen in my career, I feel I have to amend what she said. The only thing that's worse than not being published is not being published by an independent press.

About the Author

Lev Raphael is the author of sixteen books, including a short story collection, *Dancing on Tisha B'Av*, and the novels *Winter Eyes* and *The German Money*, which was a Jewish Book Council pick. Raphael has also been published widely in the Jewish press for twenty years. He speaks throughout North America, Europe, and Israel at dozens of Jewish book fairs, Jewish community centers, synagogues, and universities. He lives in Okemos, Michigan.